William G Queal

The Overthrow of American Slavery

William G Queal

The Overthrow of American Slavery

ISBN/EAN: 9783744708753

Printed in Europe, USA, Canada, Australia, Japan

Cover: Foto ©ninafisch / pixelio.de

More available books at **www.hansebooks.com**

THE OVERTHROW

OF

AMERICAN SLAVERY.

CONTAINING

DESCRIPTIONS OF IMPORTANT EVENTS AND SKETCHES OF SOME OF THE PROMINENT ACTORS.

BY

WILLIAM G. QUEAL.

"He shall not fail nor be discouraged, till he have set judgment in the earth: and the isles shall wait for his law."—ISAIAH xliii, 4.

PRINTED FOR THE AUTHOR.

NEW YORK:
PHILLIPS & HUNT.
CINCINNATI:
CRANSTON & STOWE.
1885.

PREFACE.

BOOK making is new to the author of the following lines. If it be an art, he has never practiced it. If a gift, it is as yet undeveloped.

It is not unusual for a new candidate for public attention to seek an "introduction" by some one who has attained freedom of the literary domain. We have sought no herald of this kind. For an introduction to our theme we have two hundred years of oppression and four years of convulsive civil war, the memories of which have not passed from this generation. So here we shall be content with a preface.

It is quite probable that the warders who keep the gates of the highways that lead to literary preferments will not suffer us to pass. They may not even deem us worthy of a courteous refusal, but instead thereof stand with folded arms before the barred gates, and not bestow a pasing glance on the unheralded stranger. But it is possible that among the unliveried and uncrowned millions that stand without the gates there may be some to listen to our humble song.

For speaking we claim no exceptional privilege.

We waited for a master to express our thought. We heard no breath on the air. And in the silence the question came, Why not express our own thought?

The wise and thoughtful preacher of the Divine Word does not herald before his auditors the names of the apostles of unbelief. He thinks with regard to them and the cause they serve: "Let the devil do his own advertising." The unnatural son who draws his knife against the mother who gave him birth is only worthy of oblivion. So the apostles of oppression and the chiefs and heroes of civil discord should pass to the ages to come in silence. The reader will not find their names in these pages.

Neither will there be found, what is deemed by some proofs of superior merit, any open or covert sneers at the Holy Scriptures. The writer receives these writings as a partial unveiling of providential government as well as a revelation of redemption, and allusion to their teaching and illustrations from them are freely made.

One word with regard to the form of this writing. The heroic pentameter has not been essayed. With a step more easy and facile to us we have walked over the fields we have surveyed; and if any do us the honor of walking with us, we trust they will not conclude there is nothing worth seeing because they are permitted to make the journey with even and quiet step. THE AUTHOR.

TABLE OF CONTENTS.

I.—The Discovery.

Starting from port—The master—His employment—His dreams— His observations—Efforts for help—Name—The voyage— Sailors' fears—His persistence—The discovery—The new world —Its coasts, seas, possibilities.................... 13

II.—The Settlement.

Selected seed—Their enterprise—Letters—Laws—Arts—Conscience—Love of liberty—Winnowed seed—Planting and growth... 18

III.—The Poison Seed.

The patriarch Job—His accuser—The creation—The temptation— The conflict of sin and holiness—Virginia—Its position— Climate—River James—Indian tragedies—Arrival of ship— Its news—Its wares—A new invoice—The poison-drop—The seed took root..................................... 21

IV.—Preparation for the Conflict.

European wars—England and Holland—New York became an English colony—England and France—Canada taken by the English—Colonies trained in arms—Independence—Ripened fruit—New family—Colonies drawn together—Union formed— Segments of one arc—Sun and planets................ 24

V.—The Conflict Commenced.

Hebrew mother—Condition of America—Apostrophe to freedom— Home—Labors—Winckelried—Thermopylæ—Runnymede— Patrick Henry—Washington—Many conflicts—Severe battle impending—Slavery—Birth—Music pleasant—Curse on oppressor—Starved, polluted, destroyed—Curse on oppressed— Ignorance, conscience, reason, memory, will, imagination, all injured—Slavery claims self, wife, child—Freedom and slavery seek dominion over the western world................ 28

VI.—The Conflict Continued.

Continental Congress—Declaration of Independence—Jefferson— Strike out the words—Concession to slavery—Iron and clay— Congress met to form Constitution—Liberty and justice—Brave words in front—More concessions—Clay more plainly seen—

North-western territory secured for freedom—Louisiana purchased—Held for slavery—Rivals grew—Parasitic vine on tree of liberty—Partisans met in social life—Schools—Courts—Conventions—Ballot-box—Legislative halls—Conflict irrepressible—Missouri Compromise—Slavery gained a State—Freedom had a promise—Mexico—Texas—Annexation—War with Mexico—Dismemberment—Fremont in California—Gold found—Rush to California—Gold worshipers—Freedom and slavery in conflict—California golden-crowned—Robes of freedom—Discussion—Wilmot Proviso—Fallen statesmen—Compromise—Fugitive slave law.. 35

VII.—Preponderance of Slavery.

Survey of the field—Wind blowing from the South—Public sentiment changed—Fashion's laws—Commerce—Cotton is king—Colleges—*Litterateurs*—Political parties—The printing-press—Editors—Attempts to stifle discussion—Christianity—Apostrophe to the same—Work and teaching of the Saviour—Early Church—Confronts Jew, Greek, and Rome—Destroyed gladiatorial shows—Roman slavery—Has built asylums, hospitals, almshouses—Where shall Christian Church stand in battle with slavery—Her robes were soiled—A remnant left—Different sentiments—Some rent asunder—Some marched by the tune slavery blew—Appeal to the supreme powers........... 47

VIII.—The Woes and Crimes of Slavery.

Spirit of oppression incarnate—Westminster Abbey—Preacher—Explorer—His motive—Open sore—African village surprised—Burned—Aged and infant slain—Captures—March to the coast—Bought by Christian traders—Death by the way—Slaveship—Passage—Sale—Separation—Internal slave-trade—Virginia planter—High society—Slave youth—House servant—Waiting-maid—Human love—Promise of freedom—Autumn days—Father and son—Plans—Bitter words—Apoplexy—Shipwreck—Death—Deeds of freedom burned—Brother sold to Texas—Woman faded, sold—The slave-dealer—The alarm—The sale—Separation from his family—A boy for New Orleans mansion—The slave gang—Debt—Auction sale—Household wares—The people—"Stand up, George"—A lively wench—Mother and child—How separated—Distribution of an estate—Father—Sons—Merchant doctor—Wife of senator—Wife of city pastor—Death—Sale of property and people—World went bravely on—Cotton field—Cotton picking—Slave-drivers—Morning horn—The work of a day—Two visions, one of earth and sky; the other, the cotton-pickers, the judgment-seat—Their rest—Life's alternations—Ebb and flow of sea—Ocean in storm—A fric prince—An aged man threatened—Indignation—Struck by the driver—Blow in return—Terrible excitement—Council—Judgment of the court—Sabbath morning beauty and glory—Gathering of planters, drivers, and slaves—Forces of the storm—Brazen knuckles—Flight—Swamp—Birthright maintained—Cry to God—Great preacher of Kentucky—The evening meeting—The preacher's call, hush—Prayer—Assurance—Shout—Exultant song—Railroads—Monopoly of trade—Office door shut—Its trains—*Termini*—Indiana town—Two gentlemen and servant—Conversation—Henry De Mars and servant, of New Orleans—Boat for Cincinnati—Abolitionists—Servant chose to stay with his master—Press report—Left for Niagara—Arrival—Morning ride—Bridge—Thousand-dollar chattel gone—Martin Stone—The underground traveler—Methodist preacher's house—Preacher—"Shoot me, but don't betray me"—His story—Hudson River train—Albany—R. R. conductor—The Mohawk—Train of cars—Piano music—Telegraph music—Put off the train—Hare doubled on the track—Preacher the charioteer—Traveled by the under-ground—Name from Scotia Mountains—Fugitive slave catching—The Susquehanna—Wyoming massacre—Tragedy—"No use for dead niggers"—Massachusetts—Captive slave marched through Boston—South Carolina—Tilts with Massachusetts—Bludgeon argument—Little part of the dreadful story. 65

IX.—The Awakening.

Eclipse of life—Egoism—Stupor of moral sense—Clarkson—Literary prize—Challenge to a new life—Conflict—Victory—Earth's heroes—Warriors ?—Rich ?—Genius ?—Humble ones—Fathers—Widows—An angel veiled—Unsuccessful struggles—Winfield Scott—Benjamin Lundy—Lovejoy—Garrison—Wendell Phillips—Whittier—Gerrit Smith—Horace Greeley—Charles Sumner—Milton's song—Incarnate evil—Central New York—Sons of Wesley—William Hosmer—Harriet Beecher Stowe—Frederick Douglass—Sojourner Truth—Her Prayer—Antislavery conventions—Douglass's speech—Sojourner's question—The multitudes awakehing...................... 133

X.—Skirmishes of the Great Conflict.

Spread of population—Great questions decided on small areas—Slavery's attempt to nullify Missouri Compromise—What words are worth—Slavery trumpets—Freedom's bugles—Kansas kept her freedom crown—Another John Baptist—John C. Fremont—John Brown—Crises of Life—An even thread—Stranded ship—Burning house—A man—Breath of lives—Double life—Kansas experience—Harper's Ferry—Freedom's first aggressive blow—Echoes—The cross—The gibbet—Death—His coming fame................................. 154

XI.—Divine Methods of Earthly Control.

Law—Divine Architect—Matter—Mind.—Lights above—Lost world—Lost soul—Lost universe—Civilization—Golden age—Heaven—Two instruments—Holy Bible—Wondrous history—Archives of earth—Invisible worlds—Truths interwove with human history—Inseparable—Word to be preached—Fulcrum—No penalties—Functions of civil government—All law by divine authority—Wrong in place of right—Elijah—Idol gods

—Ahab—Jezebel—Famine—Divine voice and commission—Dogs licked the blood of transgressors—First king of righteousness—King of peace—Southern land...... 165

XII.—Opening of the Armed Conflict.

Sunshine—Storm—New generation—Clouds gathering—Burst of sunlight—Charleston—Sumter—Secession—General government—The flag—New flag—Flag on Sumter—Cannon mounted—April ides—Spring beauty—God of day—Firing on the flag—The results—Fiery chrism—The treason chiefs—The flag preserved.................................. 177

XIII.—Horrors and Sorrows of War.

Battle line—Battle scenes—War Olla-Podrida—Angels' wings—Machinery hall—Briarius—An army—Beautiful picture—Torn and trampled—Other hearts—Father—Wife—Widow—Maiden—Mountain home—City palace—Mingled motives—Aspiring youth—Criminal—Gold-seeker—Place-seeker—Patriots—Abolitionists—Christians—Ax at the root of the tree. 185

XIV.—Preparation of Instruments.

An acorn—Spring—Monarch of the wood—Basket on the Nile—Moses—Learned prince—Captain—Moral fiber—Waiting—Burning bush—Wonderful call—Divine legate—Leader—Lawgiver—Vision from Nebo—Abraham Lincoln—Birth—Parentage—Early years—His problems—Saratogas—What he learned—Granite foundations—Sympathy with men—"Honest Abe"—"Uncle Abe"—His person—His spirit—Opening doors—The nation's voice—Waiting months—Progress of secession—John A. Dix—Rifle bullet—Ship of State—Robbed and abandoned—Stanton, Dix, and Holt—Lincoln's farewell address to his neighbors—Lights were out—Conspirators thwarted—Change of rulers in America—Simple forms—Solemn words—Lincoln's surroundings—Cabinet—Seward—Conflict irrepressible—Higher law—Chase—His life—Opening treasure vaults—Giant cold—Stanton—Birth—Education—Heart of oak and will of rock—His master-passion—His call—The earth was moved—At the gate-way—Wells—Smith—Blair—Bates 194

XV.—The Emancipation Proclamation.

Hebrews crossed the Jordan—Their conquests stayed—Babylonish garment—Wedge of gold—The nation's labors and sacrifices in vain—Atlas—Painter—Sculptor—Orator—Poet—Sinless One—Heavy burdened—Lincoln's problems—Legal forms shriveled—The key—Inward battles—Woodman's ax—The wedge—Rail-splitter—Flashing of the steel—The vow—Cabinet meeting—Reading Emancipation Proclamation—Measured words—Sages thrilled—All agree—Declaration of Independence—New evangel—Lincoln's word of liberty—Cannon o'er rocky road—Thenceforth forever free—Electric spark—Spectroscopic lines—Bonaparte—Providence—Heaviest cannon—Morning shower at Waterloo—Heavenly powers joined with Union forces—Hundred days—Last cord cut—Bethlehem chorus—Christ walking in the storm—Freedom come—Thanks to God—Dying saint—The last shout...................... 211

XVI.—The Battle Strife Continued.

Mississippi valley—Alleghany—Ohio—Rivers from the north—Rivers from the south—Thousand miles—Father of waters—Northward two thousand miles—Westward three thousand miles — Treasures — Inhabitants — Their determinations—Streams of men—West Virginia—Kentucky—Missouri—Tennessee—Farragut—Butler—New Orleans—Vicksburg—Grant—Trojan war—Ulysses—Trained to arms—Mexico—Sword sheathed—The florist—The crown of flowers—Unconditional surrender—March on Vicksburg—Battles—Siege—Maddened mastiff—Copper-heads—Prophets of ruin—Fortress taken—Richmond challenged Washington—Blood of Massachusetts soldiers—Rivers stained—Freedom and slavery incarnate in governments and armies—Freedom's voice—Robes powder-stained—Dripping blood—Slavery hoarse, enraged, blinded—Spring of sixty-four—A new captain—Swing of conquest—Battle-line plan—Grant's lieutenants—Indian chief—Ohio judge—William Tecumseh Sherman—Early in the field—Thought crazy—One hundred miles of mountain paths—Atlanta—Brief respite—The eagle—The boatman—Dying saint—M'Allister—Union flag—Christmas gift—Thomas—Partial view 221

XVII.—Retributive Justice on Cities and Lands.

All iniquity is marked by God—Cities are centers—Eyes—Fountains—Paris is France—Charleston—Commercial empire—Treason here bubbled—Secession's fountain unsealed—Day of judgment—Vials of wrath—Blackened corse—Columbia—Sherman's soldiers—Angels of the air—Nemesis robe—Shenandoah vale—An aged man—Record of his death—Spores of blood—Dreadful harvest—Song of old John Brown—Poison plant first on the James—Slavery breeding in Virginia—Sodom grapes ripe—Judgment angels sent to Virginia—Unseen powers vindicate righteous laws..................... 237

XVIII.—Negro Soldiers: Prisoners of War.

Modern codes of war—Rebellion revolt from advancing light—Need of Negro soldiers—No quarter to be given blacks—Leaders to be hung—Fort Pillow massacre—Life velvet-robed—Parchment-covered—Southern prison—From lands of plenty—Starvation dens—Maniacs—Skeletons—God's country—Specter angels—Two boys—Playmates—Entered the service—Ruby lips—Kirby Deval—Theodore Campbell—Their oath—Cedar Creek—Saulsbury's prison—Courage—Factors of their condition—Offer of life—Satan's lie—Council of war—One came back—One went to a nameless grave—His victory contrusted with leaders of rebellion.................................... 242

XIX.—Continued Strife.

Steady motion of time—Three years of fighting—New captain—Battles of wilderness—"By left-flank, march!"—Spottsylvania—North Anna—Cold Harbor—The James crossed—Iron men in front—Summer—Autumn—Winter—Skirts of main army—Wytheville—Lynchburg—Frederick—Washington threatened—Martinsburg—Chambersburg—Phil. Sheridan—Bugle blast—Opequan—Fisher's Hill—Cedar Creek—Shenandoah cleared—Down the coast—Terry—Fort Fisher—Schofield—Wilmington—Farragut—Mobile captured—Wilson—Northern Alabama—Selma—Columbia—Chattahoochee—Mason—End is nigh—Old flag raised in the South—Boys in blue in southern towns—Muskets in black hands—Election of Sixty-four—Prophets of evil—Party gods—Hatred of blacks—Rebel triumph feared—Debt—Dead every-where—Bands of gold—Onset of freedom's millions—Nations heard the verdict—One land—Left wing of rebellion crushed.................................... 249

XX.—Final Victory—The Rejoicing.

April ides again—Blood of Teuton tribes—Grant held rebels in Richmond till Sherman clove the treason-land—Time had come—"By left flank, march!"—Union thunders—Sabbath morning—Richmond church—Messenger—The play is done—Race for life—Another Sabbath morning—Appomattox—Army of Northern Virginia cea-ed to be—"Flash! lightnings, flash!"—"Ring! joy-bells, ring!"—"Scream! engines, scream!"—"Boom! cannons, boom!"—"Wave! banners, wave!"—"Shout! freemen, shout!"—"Sing! minstrels, sing!"—"Weep! maiden, weep!"—"Blaze! beacons, blaze!"—"Shine! cities, shine!"—"Speak! patriot, speak!"—"Rest! soldier, rest!"—Let Afric's sons rejoice—Higher note—Blood hath purchased liberty.................................... 257

XXI.—Death of Lincoln.

"Hush! joy bells, hush!"—"Lincoln has fallen!"—Not fallen—Rebellion's dying struggles—Song changed—Chalky lips—Storm past—Thunder-bolt in the sunshine—The instrument—Ancient times return—Prophet—Statesman—Sage—His prophecy—One drop more—Our time's great name.......... 267

XXII.—Punishment of Rebellion.

Brigand chiefs—Smooth spoken—Coarser mold—Italian villa—The attack—Defeat—Chiefs slain—Sad story—Unseen warring forces—Ideas—State-rights—Slavery—Battle closed—White-robed justice—Guilty captains slain—New State-rights—Slavery dead—Freedom welcome every-where....... 271

PROLOGUE.

OF making books there is no end,
    And study wearies much the flesh,
But seers have said there may be found
Sermons in stones, books in the brooks;
And if from dead and senseless things
The sage can tomes of wisdom draw,
Shall not the deeds of living men,
Their pride, their passions, and their strife,
Their prayer and labors most severe,
Their hopes and fears, their joys and pain,
Afford to us the lessons wise,
To guide our feet through tangled life?
The preacher's place is to arrange
And classify the truths he finds,
And speak the same to listening men.
    Diverse the gifts; but shall the one
To whom a rush-light hath been given,
The same beneath a bushel hide,
Because 'tis not a blazing sun?

    Because the eagle, strong of wing,
Sweeps grandly through the upper air,
So far above the mountain tops;
May not the robin chirp his song,
Among the haunts and homes of men,
When winter storms have passed away?
May not his plumage cheer the eye,
While he shall fly from field to field?

The clearer vision yet may pierce
Beyond where now our eye can reach;
The lips anointed yet may tell
The story that we trembling speak,
In tones so clear that every age
Shall listen to the wondrous tale.
    But till the kingly prophet comes,
Bearing aloft his flaming torch,
We humbly speak of that we know,
And testify that we have seen,
Remembering that a little light
Shows far when all around is night.

THE
OVERTHROW OF AMERICAN SLAVERY.

I.
THE DISCOVERY OF AMERICA.

A SIGNAL-GUN boomed on the air,
   A streamer floated from the mast
   Bearing upon its silken folds
Arms of Castile and Aragon;
And answering guns resounded far,
And answering flags were lifted high.
   Three barks that lay in Palos road
Lifted their anchors from the deep,
Shook out their sails to catch the blast,
Turned their slight prows toward western seas,
Thus starting forth to find a world.

   The master, standing on the deck,
With eagle eye turned toward the West,
Has passed the acme of his life;
His locks once jet have turned to steel;
The seams are deep upon his brow—
Sorrow hath left its traces there,
And hope hath often met defeat.
   An early toiler on the sea,
He learned to love its dashing waves,
To muse of all within its depths,
To dream of all beyond the lines
Where boldest mariner had gone.

The broken branch with curious leaf,
The weeds that came from climes unknown,
The wood which was so strangely wrought,
The dusky forms, that western winds
Had stranded on the ancient shores,
All told of land beyond the sea.

And he had passed from court to court,
And converse held with kings and queens,
And councils grave had heard his plans,
And met them with their doubts and fear.
Thus baffled oft, he sought the aid
To solve the problem of the seas.
These cares have touched the outer life,
But have not bent his iron will —
Have not destroyed his faith in God ;
But prudent, firm, heroic, true,
He walks a humble, prayerful man.

The name! till then to fame unknown.
Colombo, in his native tongue ;
In Spain, where help he found, he called
It Colon, as the Spaniards do.
In hopeful youth, in learning's pride
A Latin form, Columbus, called,
Prophetic of its coming fame.
And now in Anglo-Saxon tongue,
COLUMBUS it shall still remain.

He walks his deck in thoughtful mood,
The hour he long had sought has come ;
The land is fading from his sight,
The canvas stiffens in the breeze ;
As war-horse snuffs the field afar,
As racer bounds along the track,
The ships swept forward in their course,
Still sailing toward the setting sun.
No white-winged rover of the deep

Is seen athwart their bows by day,
No friendly light is seen by night,
No signal gun, no cry for help
From those who sink beneath the waves.

 But all alone the little fleet
Sped o'er its yet untraveled track,
Till days had grown to weeks and months.
 The seamen of those fragile barks
Were only versed in inland seas,
Or hovering near frequented coasts.
 Untutored minds soon took alarm,
Portents were thick in all the air.
 Forgetting all its ancient truth,
The needle varied from the pole;
But still the master kept his path
Until, on an October night,
A watchful eye descried the light,
And when the morning sun was bright,
A new world broke upon their sight.

 These islands of a tropic sea
Were jasper gems, set to adorn
The girdle of a virgin land;
The gate-ways of a palace fair,
Through which should come, as ages pass,
Uncounted multitudes of men,
To pay their court to crowns within.
 They were the sentinels who stand
To challenge all who may approach;
And by their presence always tell,
The solid hosts are lying near.
 COLUMBUS saw the flashing gems;
He passed the temple's beauteous gates;
He hailed the sentry on the watch;
And, though the main his feet ne'er pressed,
His eye ne'er caught the mountain tops
Of the great land for which he sought,

Historic pen shall ever say,
"COLUMBUS found *America*."

The slumbering thought of the Old World
Was thrilled as by electric touch,
When through her courts, her camps, her marts
Of trade, her legislative halls,
A world long hid was first revealed:
A new discovered ancient world,
Set in its place by Him whose word
First spake created things from naught;
When morning stars rejoiced anew,
And sons of God did shout for joy,—
Here waiting for the sons of men.

And all along the ancient coast,
There poured a restless, eager throng,
Who sought distinction on the seas,
Who sought for gold and precious gems,
Who sought for conquest, kingly rule;
And in these stirring, active times,
The coast was searched from end to end.
A land so vast in its extent,
Reaching from northern frozen seas,
From caves where iceberg fleets are launched,
Down through the wide-spread temperate clime,
To torrid heats of central zone,
Where sun forgets his south decline,
And from his fiery throne on high
Pours his fierce rays directly down;
And then to temperate climes again,
Where men look northward to the sun,
Till frozen seas are reached anew.

And through this coast-line's vast extent,
Were seas, and gulfs, and bays, and roads,
And harbors, sheltered from the blasts
Of Ocean in his stormy wrath;

While through the gate-ways of the land
The mighty floods of Amazon
And Mississippi, pouring forth,
Betokened spaces vast within.
   The daring ones who passed these gates
Found wealth of soil, and rock, and mine,
And forest trees; spices and gums;
With open streams and sleeping seas
That might bear up a nation's wealth.
   And open spaces by the sea,
Where mighty cities should be built;
And traces of the seats of power
Of ancient peoples passed away.

   This land, of such resources vast,
Of possibilities so great,
Now held by feeble wasting bands,
And only waiting brain and hand
That should transform its wilderness
To fruitful fields and pleasant homes;
Should dot its seas with cities fair,
That should uncover all its mines,
Should harness streams for human use
Which now run capering to the sea.
   And virtue, skill, and industry
Should throng its vales with kingly men.

II.
THE SETTLEMENT.

THE Husbandman of all the earth
The seed selected for this field,—
Not from the nations of the world,
Which changeless dwell from age to age,
Where pictures drawn three thousand years
Clearly reveal their life to-day.

Not from the lands of high renown,
In ancient times; where pride and sloth,
Licentious and luxurious life,
Had wrought its poison in their blood,
And sinews of their vigor cut:
But from those lands of high emprise
Which held those peoples who had come
From early founts of life in van;
And waiting stood upon the shore,
For paths to open through the seas.
Nations to whom the inheritance
From earlier ages all had come,
They had the letters of the Greek;
They had the codes of Roman law;
Their toil subdued the rugged earth,
Their arms had conquered many foes;
Science had shone upon their path,
And art adorned their vigorous life.
The quickening power of Christian truth
By the reformer's giant arm
Released from thrall, and widely spread,
Was lifting up the ranks of men.

The Settlement.

These harvest fields produced the seed
With which to sow the new-found world.

The lands were sifted for this seed;
And from the mass a separate few
Were chosen for this special work.
The men who asked for warrants clear,
For rights of kings, assumed divine;
The men who held convictions deep
Of binding force of law of God;
Whose conscience could not bend or stretch,
At word of king, or pope, or priest,
But like the oak, still stood erect
Whatever winds of doctrine blew.
Men who, with variant shades of thought,
Had ever foremost one great fact,
That for themselves they must be free:
Free in the Church, free in the State,
Free in their worship, and their work,
And only bow to truth and God.
From these were winnowed, by the winds
Of persecution, every grain
Of light, of fickle, or of false,
Until was found a band of men
Of bone and muscle, nerve and blood,
Of conscience, zeal, of faith and prayer,
Such as the world before ne'er saw;
Prepared to grapple with the storms,
To brave the winter's fiercest blasts,
To war with famine and wild beasts,
Confront and conquer every foe.
Fit grain was this with which to sow
The virgin soil of a new world.

This chosen seed of living men
Was scattered on these western shores.
It nobly grew, and widely spread
From *Plymouth* and its rock-bound coast,

By Hudson and Connecticut,
By Delaware and Chesapeake,
On lands a virgin queen gave name,
And *Carolina's* sunny coasts;
Through every vale, on every plain,
On mountain side and by the sea,
Till fields were tilled and cities grew;
And what was late a forest rude
Soon bloomed with culture's ripest fruit
Of Christian Church, with books and schools,
And beauteous homes of prosperous men.

III.
THE POISON-SEED.

THE author of the ancient song
   Recorded in the Hebrew books;
   Whose burden is the mystery
Of providential government;
Which speaks of mortal griefs and pain,
With question, if such bitter woe
Could ever fall on righteous men;
Uncovers powers that sway our life.
   There was a day when sons of God
Came to present before the Lord
Themselves and their most precious gifts.
   Then came among the chosen ones
Before Jehovah's presence bright
Satan, the foe of God and man;
Came there, God's servants to accuse,
And taunt Him with their want of faith.

   The records of an earlier time,
Creation's morning, fair and bright,
When every thing that God had made
For earth or air or sea was good:
When new-born man, create in twain,
And ranking with the sons of God,
Walked in the garden of delights,
Which ravished every sense with bliss;
Crowned with imperial powers on earth
He saw Jehovah face to face,
E'en there, the fallen son of light
With subtle art came to deceive,
With hellish hate came to destroy,

To thwart the kindly will of God,
To blight the fair abode of man,
To mar the new-made life so sweet,
So rich, endowed with heavenly gifts,
And full of all celestial joys;
He came its harmonies to clash,
From man's fair brow to dash the crown
Of holiness; his soul to fill
With bitter curse and pain of sin.
 And while he waits his final doom
In conflict with the woman's seed,
Striving in vain to bruise the heel
Which soon with power will bruise his head,
There will be tares among the wheat.

 Midway upon the Atlantic coast,
Between extremes of heat and cold,
Virginia lies, climate and soil,
Mountain and river, plain and mine,
Flora and *fauna*, all combine,
Of sister States to crown her queen.
 Upon its noblest river's banks
The Saxon on these western shores
Had formed the nucleus of a State.
 The tragedies of Indian wars,
The romance of the Indian maid,
Who braved her father's anger fierce
To save her threatened lover's life,
All had transpired upon her soil.
 But earliest dangers had been past,
And brighter days of hope had dawned.
 So far removed from early friends
The settlers anxious watched the coasts
For ships, which tidings brought from home,
Like angels' visits far between.

 A sail was seen upon the sea,
And tarrying not, it passed the gates

The Poison-Seed.

Which guard the entrance to the bay,
Selecting where to find its course
It turned its prow into the James.
   Thence forward borne by rising tides,
Its sails loose flapping by its ma-ts,
It floated on its tortuous way
Until it anchored by the town.
   The ship was welcomed for its news,
It bore to many needed wares;
It also had an invoice new—
A freight of human souls for sale!
   The seed was planted here which bore
Fruitage most full of every woe.
   The gates were opened, through which passed
Unnumbered crowds with bleeding feet
To Slavery's dreadful prison-house.
   Upon the river's beauteous banks,
Whose silver waters, sweet and clear,
From mountain springs here sought the sea,
In presence of the golden sun,
The poison reached the nation's blood.
   The fatal drop, which should ferment
And fill the channels of her life,
So full of torture and distress,
Convulsions, agony extreme,
That had the actors known their work
Their hands had palsied by their side;
With shivering fear and sick at heart
They gladly would have turned away.
   The deed was done; the seed took root;
Let tares and wheat together grow
Until the day of harvest comes.

IV.

PREPARATION FOR THE CONFLICT.

MEN oft build wiser than they know;
A Providence still shapes our course;
Disaster oft o'ertakes success,
Defeat sometimes in triumph ends.
　The wars of European States
Involved their infant colonies,
Where lordly Hudson takes its way,
Breaking the Alleghany range,
And from the western plains and lakes
Opening a pathway to the sea,
Making Manhattan's shores and bays
A gate-way for the continent.
　Holland had sent her toiling sons,
And towns were built, and fields were cleared,
Her laws and governors were here,
And she designed to hold the land.

But England claimed superior right,
And claims of right, enforced by might,
Oft leads inferior right to bow.
　And English ships sailed through the seas,
And English soldiers manned the forts,
And English rulers walked the halls
Where men of Holland late had been;
New Netherlands became *New York,*
And English rule spread o'er the land.

A hundred years had passed away ;
England and France, athletes of old,
Were interlocked in war's embrace.
Canadian province, arm of France,
Was in this struggle torn away,
And England o'er her gains rejoiced.
    These conquests added to her fame
And set new stars within her crown.
    They also helped prepare the way
For her to be despoiled; bereft
Of the right arm of her great strength—
The brightest jewels of her crown.
They trained these infant States in arms,
Revealed to them their growing power.
    The sympathies of conquered States
Were turned against their conquerors.
    The power which once would have been used
To bind revolting States to thrones
Would be employed to break these bonds
And humble their victorious foe.
'T was thus success prepared defeat.

    Analogies are thick around
To tell the story we repeat.
    The genial air of opening spring
Breathes on the woodland and the dell;
Breathes on the naked orchard trees,
Stirs in the limb, stirs in the root,
Till every branch is clothed in bloom—
A pyramid of beauty bright,
A wilderness of sweet perfume.
    These juices still in restless play,
Distilled, combined with light and air,
And shaped by Nature's plastic hand,
Are quickly molded to a sphere
Not less mysterious than our globe.
    With surface tinted for the eye
And filled with rich, delicious food,

With seed for future trees within;
When ripened, leaves the parent stem.

Thus infancy dependent, weak,
Borne in a father's loving arms,
And soothed upon a mother's breast;
When years give vigor to the frame,
And use develops mental power,
Soon girds his loins with manhood's strength,
And leaves the home of early youth
Another family to build.

These colonies obeyed this law,
And they, when interests were diverse
From interests of the British crown,
Declared themselves no longer held,
But independent of her power.
And through fierce conflict many years
This declaration they maintained;
Till Britain, weary of the strife,
Acknowledged them as sovereign States;
Allegiance to her crown dissolved,
Free to perform all sovereign arts,
Free to control their own concerns,
And by their own internal force
To shape their future destiny.

These States, by common danger joined,
Found need, when foreign war had passed,
Of union, closer, more direct
Than laws and treaties changing oft
Could give. To meet this new-found want
A government was formed; complete
In all its parts, united, free,
Elective, stable, guarded powers,
Returning oft to those who gave;
Segments united in one arc
The separate rays of light conjoined

To blend again in perfect white ;
The sun, whose strong attraction binds
The planets in appointed spheres,
Diffusing light and heat and life
To all who in their orbits keep.

   These lands so highly blessed of God,
In climate, soil, in sea and shore,
In government, in laws and arts,
In civil and religious rights,
Were now left free their course to take;
To demonstrate the power of man
To live upright, subject alone
To God's eternal, righteous laws.

V.

THE CONFLICT COMMENCED.

TWO nations are within thy womb;
   Two peoples shall from thee go forth;
   The struggles of their embryo state
Reveal the conflicts of their life.
To soothe the ancient mother's fears,
Was thus explained, at her request,
The secret of her tortured womb.

   And thus *America* has found.
The lives which quickened by her blood
In currents ran diverse from each.
   The firstborn, FREEDOM, fair and true,
Has struggled long with SLAVERY.
And many years, it might be said,
The elder doth the younger serve.

   O, Freedom! Spirit of the air,
Brooding in silence o'er the lands,
Waiting the genesis of sons.
   Thy home is in the mountain-tops,
Conversing with the clouds and storms,
And where majestic forests stretch—
Whose mighty trunks and giant limbs
Withstand the fierce tornado's blast—
Where rivers roll mid mountain crags,
And cataracts dash and thunders roar.
   Thou'rt also found mid rural scenes,
Where men hold converse with the earth,
Hearing the whispers of her voice
In rains and dews and trickling streams;

Seeing the beauty of her robes
In summer grasses, forest leaves,
In winter snows and frost fringed groves,
In clouds with which she veils her face,
And fruits and flowers that gem her brow.

Thou standest in the senate halls
Where men speak not with bated breath,
But free discussion rules the hour.
Thou art a brother born, of light,
The parent of the printing-press,
The flashing lightning's iron pen.
And every voice that speaks for truth,
And every sigh for liberty,
And every blow at tyrant's chains,
Have been begotten by thy breath.

Thy spirit dwelt among the Alps
When patriotic Winckleried,
To break the Austrian soldiers' ranks,
Swift forward rushed, and in his arms
Gathered a sheaf of poisoned spears;
"Make way for liberty!" he cried;
"Make way for liberty!" and died.
Thy spirit at Thermopylæ
Checked Xerxes, and his Persian host,
Giving such ardor to the Greek
That he could die, but could not flee.
Thy spirit nerved the British arms
That, in the vale of Runnymede,
Did win from a reluctant king
The *Magna Charta* of their rights.
Thou hast inspired the poet's songs.
Thou touched the patriot's lips with fire,
When in the ardor of his soul,
With outstretched arm and flashing eye,
And voice of thunder-tone he cried:
"To me give liberty or death."

Thy spirit moved Columbia's son,
The great immortal WASHINGTON.

The records of the ages past
Thy conflicts tell in many fields.
Defeated oft, by might struck down,
Bleeding and faint, but not destroyed;
With battle scarred, with crimson stained,
The work thou hast to do undone
Bequeathed from bleeding sire to son.

And yet, thine eye still keeps its fire,
Thy brow is open, fair, serene,
Thy feet are ready still to march,
Thy hand is resting on the hilt,
For the defense of trampled right,
For the relief of prisoned souls.

But Freedom! battle's gage is thrown
In this fair land by pilgrims trod,
And never in thy ancient strife
Hast thou been called to such a work
As presses now upon thy hand.
Gird up thy loins and grasp thy sword.
The contest is for liberty
For many millions yet to be.
The wager is the nation's life,
Periled by Slavery's poisoned breath.
The conflict is for souls redeemed;
For freedom bought by precious blood.
For truth of the eternal word.
Spotless to keep the throne of God
From charge of fellowship with sin.
Gird up thy loins, and draw thy sword;
Thy scabbard hath no longer use.

SLAVERY! child of sinful birth,
Begotten by the evil one,
And fed on pride and luxury,

On indolence and love of power,
On greed of gold, and fleshy lust:
To such proportions vast has grown
It claims dominion of the earth.
  And those that to this Moloch bow
Senseless become to human woe.

  Their ears find music in the chains
Which clank upon the bondman's arm,
In rusted hinges grating harsh
On prison doors and dungeon cells,
Where darkness and despair abide.
  The moans and sighs of broken hearts,
The agonies of childless ones,
Bereft by Slavery's murderous hands,
Disturb them not. No eye to see,
No ear to hear, no hand to save
The souls despoiled by Slavery's power:
The curse of this malignant fiend
Rests on oppressor and oppressed;
'T is hard to say which suffers most.

  The oppressor has his conscience seared,
His reason jostled from its throne;
No high endeavor for the right,
No sacrifice to save the weak,
By which a man allies himself
To Him who came the lost to save.

  In place of these high qualities
There is enthroned the love of self.
  The passions have unbridled rein;
The will, gigantic in its power,
Brooks no dissent from its high claim,
Nor bows to man, nor bows to God.
  And soul and body bear the marks
Of Slavery's foul polluting touch,
Like murderous Cain in justice set.

No tongue can tell, no mind conceive,
The awful depths where Slavery leads
The souls who take his damning bribes.

While thus the oppressor wears his chain
The souls oppressed are also crushed;
No knowledge comes to light their path,
To them the Book of God is sealed;
The crowning work of God on earth,
The human soul, with breath of lives,
Conscience, reason, memory, will,
Is a sealed tomb. The dead are there;
The stone is rolled upon the door.
The balance nice of moral sense,
Which, when adjusted to its place,
Doth rule among the faculties,
As sun controls the rolling spheres:
The reason ; made for noble work,
To trace the laws of God on earth
Through every form of active force ;
From truths of divers texture, fair
To build her palaces of thought,
Where wearied souls may rest in peace;
With lines and angles to erect
A stair-way reaching through the skies,
Where students of the universe
May safely walk from star to star,
And in her work, conjoined with faith,
May reach e'en to the eternal throne,
And with Jehovah converse hold:
Memory; whose expansive shelves
And spacious alcoves, reaching high,
Have room for cabinets of art,
And tomes of history and law;
With books of science manifold,
And records of affections true ;
Which make the chambers of the soul
A gallery of every age:

The will; calm-seated on her throne,
Or rising up and going forth,
By conscience and by reason's light;
Self-moving like the dreadful wheels,
In vision of the ancient seer;
Imagination's flashing wing
Which scales the loftiest heights of song;
And music, with her voice divine,
In harmony with seraph strains:—
All these lie crushed within the breast,
And only conscious to the slave
By the dull pain their presence gives.

 These nobler faculties of soul
Repressed and crushed, its forces turn
To other channels for their flow;
Conjugal and parental love—
The fountains whence so many draw
The richer, sweeter joys of life.
 As slave, he has no house or lands,
No gold or diamonds, precious store,
No works of art, no book or pen,
No time to train the humblest thought;
But God hath made a helpmeet true,
Bone of his bone, flesh of his flesh:
To each to cleave till death shall part;
And little ones whose loving touch
The parent thrills, and tendrils live
Are interlashed and intertwined,
Through every fiber of the heart.
 And while no other good they hold,
Sure they may keep their wife and child?

 But Slavery says, "Your wife is mine,
For any purpose that I choose;
Mine for my service, when I wish;
Mine for my lust, if that I will;
Mine for the lash when she offends;

Mine in her youth, and mine when old,
And mine for sale when I need gold."
   And Slavery says, "Your child is mine;
To beat or bruise, to feed or starve,
To keep or sell; and, at my will,
To tear it from its parents' arms,
And send it ever from their sight."

   And when the tendrils of their love
Asunder snap, and broken cords
Are bleeding in their bosoms left;
Then putrefaction of the soul
Begins and spreads through all its life,
And every noble impulse dies.
   Revenge and hate, malignant, fierce,
Deceit and falsehood, cruel, sly,
Malice, and murder enter in
The soul to torture, there abide.

   These champions of good and ill
Again have met, and face to face
Alert they stand, while Slavery seeks
Dominion o'er the western world.

VI.
THE CONFLICT CONTINUED.

THE fathers of these States had met;
The fierce collision of the strife
With parent State had grown to war.
Concord and *Lexington* were wet
With patriot blood. England, aroused,
Was putting on her giant strength
Rebellion swift in blood to crush,
And give the chiefs of this revolt
Before the world a felon's doom.
In England's triumph, every hand
Their own death-warrant had subscribed.
Surrounded by these solemn scenes
Which burdened every thought, they penned
The charter of the nation's life.
" We hold," say these immortal words,
" These truths to be self-evident,
That equal men are all create;
And by their Maker each endowed
With these inalienable rights:
The right to life, to liberty,
And the pursuit of happiness."
And thus there rings through every line
A voice for freedom, strong and clear.

Fit words were these from pen of him
Who said, " In case of servile war,
God hath no attribute to join
The oppressor, in his fiendish work;
Remembering that God is just,

I tremble for my country's weal;
Justice will not forever sleep."
  Thus wrote *Virginia's* foremost son,
The great immortal JEFFERSON.
He further said, " The British crown
Refused assent to wholesome laws,
Designed to check the trade in slaves;
And purpose shows to bind on us
The curse and shame of slavery."

  But Slavery said, "Strike out these words,
We can't allow an inference clear
That we desire to free the slave."
And so the words were stricken out.

  Brave words for freedom in the front,
For liberty and equal rights
Concession made to Slavery's claim
Before completion of the work;
Mingling the iron and the clay,
In the Republic's corner-stone.

But record make unto the praise
Of the immortal names affixed
To this evangel of our rights,
No word implies a single slave.
  Another fact should still be told:
The patriots of those early days
Thought slavery swiftly must expire
Under the blaze of freedom's light;
And in the ages yet unborn
These shining words, without a flaw,
Shall stand a beacon for the free.

Again the patriot fathers met;
The storm of war had left the skies,
And bow of peace was shining there.

They met to frame organic law;
A Constitution to ordain,
Perpetual union to secure,
Justice establish in the land;
And for their sons through unborn time
Liberty's blessings to secure.

And for these high and worthy ends
They say, in solemn reverent tone,
The People, We, of these free States,
This Constitution do ordain,
And it establish evermore.
Brave words again stand in the front;
Liberty and justice were the ends
This instrument was made to guard.
And yet provision still is made
For "persons, who to service held"
They may be numbered, but in part
When laws are framed, or taxes laid,
The law may not forbid import
For given time. When they escape,
None shall forbid delivery back.
And thus with much circuitous phrase,
To save the mention of the name,
The charter of a nation free
Is stained with foot-prints of this crime.
The iron mingled with the clay,
The clay now more distinctly seen.

With freedom, peace, and stable laws
There quickly came increase of power.
The people multiplied and spread;
The denizens of lands oppressed
Thronged swiftly to these open doors.
The forests fled at their approach,
And homes and towns sprang in their path.

Beyond Ohio's rolling floods
A wilderness of wealth was found.

Forests and plains, with rivers, seas,
And richest soils, with woods and mines,
Unrivaled on the rolling earth :
   And Freedom said, These lands are mine.
   And at her word the laws were made
To keep this soil forever free—
And under her inspiring breath
These forest glades and plains were changed
To empires, filled with toiling men.
   Where Mississippi's swelling floods,
Gathered from spaces far remote,
And draining half a continent,
Debouches to the open sea,
Another nation held its claim.
   For varied reasons this was bought;
For it was paid the nation's gold;
It had unmeasured lines and bound,
Far stretching toward the setting sun ;
And Slavery overspread these lands
And claimed unblushing for her own.
   Thus side by side these rivals grew,
And each more strong than other knew.

   And thus the hopes of patriot sires,
That freedom should erelong outgrow
And cast away from living tree
This dangerous parasitic vine,
Had come to naught. This fungus growth,
Covering entire the southern side,
And piercing every branch and root
With poisoned filament, to draw
The life-blood from its veins away,
Revealed the fact: that time might come
When Freedom, standing still erect,
With outward semblance left of life,
That life should lose; and only be
A crumbling column, standing whiles
For the support of Slavery.

The soldiers of these rival ranks
On many fields of battle met;
In the arene of social life,
In academic tilts and frays,
In courts where counselors were matched,
Upon the platform for debate
Where men discussed the public need;
In synods, and assemblies wise,
Where Christian teachers often spoke
Of claims of God, of rights of man;
Or else said, with obsequious lips,
"Servants, ye must your masters serve,"
And gathering in convention halls,
To mold the shapes of nascent States,
To form the party's platform deft
And name the candidate, to win
The spoils of office and of power:
These subjects, oft repressed, arose
The conflict irrepressible.

But chiefly at the ballot-box,
And in the legislative halls,
Where finished products of the strife
Are coined into the nation's laws;
We hear the thunder of the shock,
And see the flashing of the steel.
A field-day of this constant war
Occurred, when, with her forms prepared,
Missouri came to take her place
Beside her sister States a peer;
Beyond the Mississippi tides,
Opening the occidental gates.
She came with fundamental laws
To cover holding men in chains.

For months within the Congress halls
The conflict raged. And men of might

Answered the southern fallacies,
And for their strokes gave blow for blow.
  The contest closed with compromise.
—A baleful word first introduced.—
Slavery took the immediate wage,
To Freedom future promise given.
  A line was drawn, and northern lands
By solemn ordinance was declared
To Freedom ever consecrate.
  The State received by compromise
Gave added strength with which to break
The seals of Freedom's covenant.

  A little rest, and then again
Fresh turmoil from this conflict rose.
  Upon our western borders lay
A land with territory vast;
Republic, federal, like our own,
Its peace with many factions vexed
And torn; yet, true to liberty,
Its laws forbade the holding slaves.

  Texas, its farthest eastern State,
Refused consent to Freedom's laws,
And raised the standard of revolt.
  She also sought with sudden haste
To join the north *United States*.
  Freedom still uttered her protest,
But Slavery, proud and arrogant,
Rapacious and exultant grown,
Holding the reins of civil power,
With short, impetuous, quick resolve,
Annexed the late revolted State;
And also war with *Mexico*.
  Upon the balance, added weight
To Slavery's fast-increasing power.
  The war annexed was sternly fought
Until the faction-rended State,

Humbled and broken by defeat,
Consented to dismemberment;
Which gave vast States to conquering foe.

The careful student of events,
Who shall survey in after-time
This drama's acts in all its scenes,
This acquisition, will declare
To be beginning of the end.
Another proof of adage old:
Whom gods destroy they first make mad.

Those earnest, restless, moving men,
Whose dwelling-place is just beyond,
What has already been attained;
Like Macedonian conqueror,
Forever seeking other worlds,
Before the war with *Mexico*
Had camped on the Pacific coast.
The sound of war was in the air;
They heard its thrilling tones afar,
And quick to do, and brave to dare,
They took possession of the land.
The finder of the mountain paths,
FREMONT, the leader of the band.
And thus their acts prepared the way
For the new masters to have rule.

A settler toiling at his work,
Digging the race for needed mill,
Where waters washed the graveled bed,
He saw, among its glittering sand,
Some shining particles of gold.

Ho! ho! for *California!*
The land is found of poet's dream;
El Dorado—promised land,
Where waters run o'er golden sand;

Where clay is flecked with yellow ore,
Where rocks are seamed with golden gleams,
Where mountain peaks their nuggets keep,
Where mines are rich and broad and deep.
And gold in every form is found;
Which only waits the willing hands
To gather in its precious store.
 Ho! ho! for *California*, come!
And thus the shout went ringing out,
Ho, all! for *California*, come!

O! wondrous human thirst for gold,
The master-passion of the heart,
What tongue can tell its giant strength?
 Its devotees fill every clime,
And compass earth to win its smile.
 No altars or high-priests it hath,
No temples for its public praise;
And yet it has what God demands,
The truthful homage of the heart;
And 'mid its throng of worshipers
There ne'er was found a hypocrite.

 To gratify this burning thirst
Men toil in pain from youth to age.
 They clothe themselves in cast-off rags,
And starve and freeze to save their gold.
 They trample on the widows' rights,
And orphans rob t' increase their store.
 They take their neighbor's wealth by fraud;
They rob the treasury of the State;
They sell their country's dearest rights;
They leave their place of birth, their home,
To circumnavigate the earth,
To dwell in tropic climes, to scale
The mountain height, the rivers ford,
To delve in mines, to starve in wilds,
To be consumed both day and night

By drought and moisture, cold and heat,
And all for gold, for shining gold.
  Yea more, they wash their hands in blood
Of murdered men, and on their brow
The mark of crime forever bear.
  And in their souls, tormenting fiends
Accuse, recriminate, and taunt,
And scorpion stings within them burn,
The prelude to the judgment fires—
And all for gold, for shining gold.

  Not strange, this voice resounding far,
Bidding the multitude to come
And freely take abundant wealth,
With golden fruit their baskets fill,
That many heard and rashly rushed
To slake with gold their burning thirst.

  All ranks of men were in this throng:
The farmer left his plow afield,
The artisan locked up his shop,
The banker shut his counting-house,
The merchant left his silken wares,
The counselor laid down his briefs,
Physicians left their patients' side,
The lumberman forgot his ax,
And fisherman forsook his net;
The student left his college halls,
The printer laid aside his stick,
And writer quick laid down his pen.
  The ministers of truth were moved;
Some went to drown the voice of God,
And gather up the shining dust;
And some to stand beside the way
And cry to thronging multitudes:
Wisdom is better far than gold.
  There also came the cormorants,
Who seek their spoils where throngs are found:

The vender of the cup of death,
The gambler and the debauchee,
The assassin and the midnight thief,
The wanton, with her brazen face,
Whose house the steps lead down to hell;
And when a few short months had passed,
This restless, mingled, seething stream
Debouched upon the golden shore.

   Freedom is mobile, quick to start;
Her limbs unbound, her muscles lithe,
Like flying armament in field
Her men can mount and dash away,
Dismount, unlimber, prime her guns,
And train them on her startled foes.
   Her scouting parties swiftly ride
O'er mount and plain, from burden free,
And forage what their needs require.
   Slavery is slow, with leaden foot,
She, burdened, moves to distant lands.
   Like army, with a heavy train,
Baggage, provision, and pontoon,
And cattle droves with dogs and guards,
Which army needs for their advance,
And needs an army to protect.
   So driving human chattels, far
Beyond the law and social pact,
There comes the danger of stampede.
   Thus Freedom had the vantage-ground
On *California's* golden fields.

   Man needs for his defense the law;
Brutes cluster in gregarious herds,
Without despoil of others' rights;
But man, with higher gifts endowed,
Can sink to lower depths of wrong;
He takes besides the good he needs
What to his neighbor doth belong,

And therefore needs restraint of law,
And penal judgment on his crimes.

And thus the men who sought for gold
Soon found the need of law's defense.
Convention of the people framed
The charter to secure their rights.
And *California*, golden crowned,
With Freedom's vestal robes adorned,
And maiden bloom upon her brow,
Was knocking at Columbia's gates
Beside her sisters to have place.

Before the nation's rulers came
The ever-rising theme again.
When terms were made with Mexico,
And large possessions from her torn,
Then Freedom's representative,
WILMOT, of *Pennsylvania*,
Proposed that never " servitude,
Except for crime," should blot that land.
For weeks and months this simple clause
Was fought within the Congress halls,
And through the land the battle raged.
The myrmidons of Slavery,
Who forced the war with *Mexico*,
And then despoiled her broad area
To wider spread their cherished shame,
Saw failure shadowing their designs.
Then rage and anger knew no bounds.
With varied threatenings they declared,
Unless they were allowed the right
To carry slavery through the land,
The Union temple, wisely built
By patriot sires, they would destroy.
And in the nation's capitol
The fierce conflicting currents met;
And while they rushed and boiled and foamed,

Some were alarmed, and safety sought
By yielding to these vengeful threats.
  And some, who many years had stood
As standard-bearers of the free,
By presidential hopes were dazed,
And footing lost, ignobly fell
From envied heights to rise no more.

  The conflict closed with compromise.
  The golden State which had eschewed
The curse of slavery from her soil
Into the Union was received.
  The new possessions organized
Were left without the shield of law
To save them from the oppressor's hand.
  And, worst of all, the once free North
Was made anew a hunting ground,
Where fleeing fugitives were caught,
And thrust beneath their chains again.

VII.
PREPONDERANCE OF SLAVERY.

WITH varying fortunes through the years,
   Freedom and Slavery, face to face,
   The conflict waged. Nor either fought
Without sometimes a battle lost.
   Appropriate now to calm survey,
The progress either cause has made.

   Two hundred thirty years have passed
Since seed of slavery first was dropped
In virgin soil of western world;
A century has three quarters gone
Since independence was achieved.
   The nation stands now near midway
The nineteenth century, of Him
Who came earth's galling yokes to break.
   The call, "Watchman, what of the night?"
Must still have answer, night prevails,
And only eye of seer can see
The morning cometh on apace;
Around is darkness all and gloom.
   But still the shining stars aloft
Keep onward in their wondrous way.
The world is turning toward the sun,
Which shall disperse the clouds of wrong;
And introduce that better earth,
Where righteousness and peace shall dwell.
   But eyes of men are holden still,
They do not know their Master's walk.

Philosophers of modern time
Have promulgated this decree:
"Nature a vacuum abhors;"
They say she fills her spaces all,
With earth and air, with light and heat,
With ether and electric fire,
Enfolding and infilling all.
  So wrapped around each mortal life,
And entering in through all its ways,
An essence, subtle, undefined,
Unmeasured, and intangible,
Prevails; a public sentiment.
  Like wind that bloweth where it lists,
We scarce can tell from whence it comes,
On what it lives, or how it grows,
But still it has a real force,
And few withstand its potent sway.
  In early time this healthful wind,
Came from the clear and bracing North,
With Freedom's perfume richly lade;
And by its aid, with little law,
The northern skies from clouds were cleared.
  So healthful this inspiring breath,
The patriot and philanthropist,
The judge, the statesman, and divine,
All looked to see the lingering clouds,
Relic of ancient barbarous times—
From Freedom's skies forever swept.

  But when eternal vigilance,
Which is the price of liberty,
Was for a little time relaxed;
While arms were stacked and laurels wore,
Unnoticed came a change. Behold!
The winds of public sentiment
Were blowing from the farther South,
Laden with Slavery's fetid breath.
  And with this air intoxicate

The people soon began to crouch,
And some went staggering through the land,
While others groveled in the dust,
Soiling in filth a freeman's robes,
And eating dirt, as Southrons bade.
  So long this baleful wind had blown,
Bearing its poisonous odors north,
That faintness overspread the land.

  There are departments in our life
As rulers have, who execute
The laws with which they are intrust;
A life of labor or of ease,
A life of sickness or of health,
A life of poverty or wealth,
A life adorned with learning's lore,
Or else by ignorance depressed;
A life with home affections crowned,
Or barren of domestic joy;
A life of good or life of ill,
As man obeys his Maker's will.

  Amid these mingled, varying forms,
No laws demand more careful heed,
Than Fashion claims in social life.
  'Tis not a witless play of words
Which light declares, "As well be dead
As out of fashion's" coterie.
  This fickle goddess reigns a queen
From inner circle; *crême de crême.*
  Her mandates issued from the throne,
All classes bow at her behest,
On pain of severance from her court.
  Her laws regard all earthly things:
Our dress, our pleasure, church, and school,
The conversation we may hold,
The place of sojourn at the springs,
Or ocean side, or mountain air.

She measures out the mincing step,
And pendants hangs upon the ears.
  She times the utterance of a sigh,
And leave imparts to shed a tear;
She gives the hues to tinge the face,
And shapes the frizzle of the hair.

  As Islam follower turns his face
To sacred Mecca when he prays,
So Fashion's devotees all turn
Toward their goddess' inner shrine,
Whence her commands are issued forth.
  Alas! 'tis true, they often find
Her court is but an empty place,
And crowns and thrones are only gilt.
  Like other vaunted mysteries,
Which earnest sought, they only yield
A labyrinth of opening doors;
Within, no sacred holy place,
Where stones engraved, and budding rod,
And gifts of heavenly bread are kept,
Much less divine Shekinah's flame.

  But still the goddess subjects hath,
Who follow blindly all her whims;
  And Fashion said, in dulcet tones,
'Tis very vulgar to regard
The weal or woe of colored men.
  She talked of an inferior race,
Bearing their Maker's brand of wrath.
  Not strange that those who turn away,
At Fashion's strange absurd behest,
From children of their flesh and blood,
At Fashion's nod should soon forget
The sorrows of the lowly born.

  So after the heroic days,
When Freedom walked a prince, had passed,

And Slavery, with imperious step,
With courtly grace and polished air,
With gold and gems ornate adorned,
The price of sweat and toil enforced—
Had bowed to Fashion, reigning queen,
She quickly smiled in glad response.
And soon the twain joined arm and arm,
Together walked from South to North,
Through social centers of the land,
And all the ranks of social life
Submissive bowed to Slavery.

Cities are centers vast of wealth,
Of social and commercial power,
Which run along the lines of trade,
As heart sends blood through artery
To nourish and maintain our life.
And blood corrupt in any part
Will find its way, through central heart,
To every member of the frame.

The cities are the open gates
Through which are sent, from all the lands,
The multitudinous results
Of labor, fancy, art, and skill;
And in her palaces are stored
Commodities of all the earth.
Like ancient Babylon, they have
The gold and silver merchandise,
The precious stones, the pearls, the silks,
The purple and the scarlet wool,
The precious wood and ivory,
And forms of marble, iron, bronze,
And cinnamon and odors sweet,
Ointments and frankincense and wine,
And oil and flour and wheat and beasts,
And sheep and horses, chariots grand,
And purchased slaves, and souls of men.

Their merchants glorify themselves
And live deliciously. Thy say,
Our only business is to trade,
To buy and sell and gather gain.
In this no North or South we know,
No right or wrong, no good or ill,
But customers and trade we seek.
To sell our goods we sell ourselves
And only speak as others choose.

So when the pompous cotton lords
Rehearsed the wealth of cotton lands,
And numbered o'er their chattels owned,
And told the gold that cotton brought,
Then cried aloud, "Cotton is king!"
Merchants replied, "Cotton is king!"
And when they cried, "Long live the king!"
The merchants said, "Long live the king!"
And then through all the lines of trade,
Canal and river, iron road,
The cry went forth through all the land:
"Cotton and Slavery jointly reign,
Behold the king! Long live the king!"

And thus through our commercial life
The virus of oppression spread.
Some few there were who dared reply,
When asked at Slavery's shrine to bow,
"Our goods are at the market price,
Our principles are not for sale;"
But most, without protest or blush,
Bowed down at the oppressors' word.

There is a guild of learned men,
Thus called, from being taught in schools,
And bearing titles from the same.
And many worthy are to hold
A brotherhood of this degree;

While some have only parchment scrolls,
Showing their term at college halls.
This order hath its institutes,
And masters, with their ancient forms;
It also hath its interests
Pertaining to the present time.
  It money needs, its chiefs to pay,
And keep its temples in repair.

  And when the crowds of earnest youth
Came from the southern sunny land
To Learning's temples in the North,
Their hands well filled with needed gold,
No words were used to give offense
To sons of southern chivalry,
Lest the abundant golden stream
Should through these channels cease to flow.

  And thus the class which should be first
To loosen man from every thrall,
To rend the fetters from his limbs,
And darkness from his mind dispel,
Was hindered in its noble work;
But, Samson-like, in prison kept
With blinded eyes, was called to grind
The meal which Slavery wished to use.

  Another literary guild,
The fancies of whose fertile brain
Kindly supplied the insatiate maw
Of millions waiting to be fed,
Whose books fell thick as autumn leaves
In classic *Valombrosa's* vale,
And like the Egyptian plague of frogs,
Were found in chamber, parlor, hall,
In kitchen and in kneading-trough;
Which ever spake of loves and hates,
And joys and griefs, with many things

Ne'er probable nor possible,
They hardly dared to breathe a word
Against the crimes of Slavery,
But strewed their fancies o'er the same,
As flowers are brought to deck a corpse,
And hide from sight Death's dreadful work.

In an elective government
Electors join in party ranks
As freezing waters crystals form,
Or falling rains in myriad drops
Complete the arch which crowns the sky.
These parties serve important ends,
Combine divergent thoughts and aims,
And thus secure the public weal.
When those in power abuse their trust,
Opposing parties criticise,
And either check their froward way,
Or hurl them from their seats of power.
Abuse of party is to seek,
By party pride and drill, to place
Corrupt and base in seats of trust.
Or else by deftly chosen words,
Which, framed to read in either sense,
Retains its followers in its ranks,
And by deceit secures success.
These parties instruments employ,
And chief among them is the press.

The crowning triumph of our age,
Combining greatest human skill,
With richest product of the thought—
The true and real microcosm—
Is the damp sheet which softly drops
From fingers of the printing-press.
The mightiest force that man controls
Is used to do this matchless work.
The chemist, with retort and fire,

In just proportion wisely sought
The varied metals to combine,
To make the bit of shining type;
Then formed a mold where molten fire
Congealed to rock; then mingled ink,
Which, touching every upturned face,
Could be transferred to virgin page.

   Subtle invention pondered long,
And oft with vain experiment,
To so combine the wheels and disks,
Levers and arms and joints and bands,
Revolving cylinders and plates,
And fonts for ink, and spreading rolls,
With iron fingers moving free,
To grasp and loose with rapid touch,
To lift the tender moistened sheet
And place it subject to such power
As works the mines, or draws the train;
To drop it from the iron kiss
Untorn, unworn, unsoiled, complete.
   The work was done. The human mind
Evoked from naught the power press.
   From North and South, from East and West,
By mail, express, and telegraph,
Is gathered news from all the earth.
Reports from men who make the laws,
The arts of cabinets of State,
The flow of trade, the price of stocks,
The movements of the railroad trains,
And steamers on their ocean trips;
Convention, court, and conference,
The news of club and church and school;
The various accidents and crimes,
The wedding *fêtes*, the births and deaths,
The storms, the crops, the health and wealth,—
All these and more, as oft 'tis said,
Too numerous to mention now,

By subtle brains and careful hands,
Assorted, sifted, and compiled,
Are deftly wrought to daily news,
Which papers gather and diffuse.

   The editor in chief controls
The public tone his sheet shall bear.
   He writes the leaders, and confers
With party chiefs. He takes the note
Of owner's bent, and studies well
Political thermometers,
And barometric altitudes,
To learn the ways of winds and storms,
That he may turn his waiting sails
To catch whatever currents blow,
And day by day and week by week
This mighty engine to instruct,
Control, direct, and stimulate,
Is sent abroad through all the land;
And press and party walk abreast
In every question of the time.

   Two parties sought the ruling place.
From time to time each lower stooped,
Till both agreed that States once free
Should be a hunting place for men.
   Then each in council grave resolved
To frown, resist, and deprecate,
Every attempt to agitate
The questions which concern the slave;
And party press responded, "Aye,
These questions shall forever down."

   O Church of Christ! thy holy name
Should always stand a beacon-light
To humble, poor, and suffering man.
   Thy Founder built his throne on love,
A rock that never shall be moved.

The sword shall lose its brilliant glare,
And all its conquests be unknown.
  The pen shall palsy in its course,
And sleep with ancient heroes past;
Its builded fancies all dissolved.
  The glittering gold shall slowly rot,
And be to man but yellow clay;
But love shall stand for evermore.

  And when the great Eternal One,
Who spake from naught the heavenly hosts
By his almighty forming word,
Came to our earth, to win again
Apostate children, wandered far,
And build on Sin's demolished throne
Immortal temple for his praise,
He laid the first foundation-stone
In toiling, suffering, dying love.
  His crown and scepter laid aside,
The blinding light now veiled in flesh,
He walked in lowly human homes,
Dispensing good where'er he went.
  Diseases vanished at his touch,
Wrong hid, affrighted, from his gaze;
Death, listening to his wondrous voice,
Returned the spoils he late had won,
And mourning hearts were comforted.

  He gave commission: "Heal the sick,
The lepers cleanse, and raise the dead;
Freely ye have received from me,
And freely give to all that need."
  He told of one who, robbed and torn,
Neglected by the scribe and priest,
A neighbor found in ancient foe,
Who healed, protected, saved the man.
  And then he said: "When ye shall find
The robbed and crushed and bleeding ones,

Go ye and likewise do to them,
And be a true Samaritan."
A golden rule his lessons crowned:
"Whate'er you would men do to you,
E'en so to others must ye do."

He loved his own unto the end;
Excused the weakness of the flesh
When watchers slumbered at their posts.
With words of kindness he received
"Hail, Master!" and betraying kiss;
With look of utmost love he broke
Unfaithful Peter's guilty heart;
And sealed his love for sinners lost
By drinking Death's sin-poisoned cup.

The teaching, healing, life, and death,
Of wondrous Man of Nazareth;
His supplemental gift of power,
Whose flaming touch at Pentecost
Filled the disciples' souls with love,
And gave them tongues of hallowed fire,
Prepared his servants for their work.
Anointed thus he sent them forth
To preach the Gospel to the poor,
Deliverance to the captives bring,
Unto the blind their sight to give,
To set at liberty the bruised.
To preach the Lord's accepted day,
The reign of righteousness and truth,
Of peace on earth, good-will to men.
O Church of Christ! the chosen one
Empowered to speak on earth for him,
Who hence shall speak in heaven for thee;
Be faithful in thy Master's work.

The visions of the ancient past
Are rising upward to our view.

The melodies of Christian songs
Come murmuring down the stream of time.
The Church of Christ with girded loins
Is pressing onward in her work.
With law and prophets in her hands,
Which point to David's greater Son,
She soon confounds the scribe and priest.
She meets the wisdom-seeking Greek
With science that has power to save.
Within the ancient Parthenon,
Where gods of every clime are found,
She there proclaims the Eternal One,
And Jesus Christ whom he hath sent.
She enters Rome's imperial courts,
And dares confront her mighty chiefs
Who bear from conquered lands the spoils
Of gold and art and captive slaves.

Within her theaters she saw
The gladiators fierce and strong,
And trained to do this dreadful work,
Each other strike and rend and pierce,
Till human flesh was quivering gore;
While senators, nobles, maidens fair,
Patrician, plebeian, all degrees,
By thousands chanted and rejoiced,
And relished well this hellish feast.

She also saw the lions steal
On captive youth, or beauteous maid,
On criminal of high degree,
Or Christian who would not blaspheme;
And soon the human form divine
Was smeared with blood, broken and crushed;
Limb torn from limb, and entrails flung
From side to side, while shouts and songs
Went up from those whom scenes like these,
From men, had changed to living fiends.

With tongue of fire and heart of love,
The Church of Christ this work forbade.
And though her words her sons exposed
To flames and lions, ax and sword,
She persevered, nor turned aside
Until this hellish work had ceased;
Till Cæsar's throne had bowed to Christ,
Till Christian life did permeate
The lands that bowed to Roman sway,
And Christian love had melted off
The chains that held the bondman's limbs.

And what if in a later age,
Contending for the forms of words,—
The robes of doctrine which she wears,—
She for a time forgot her work:
She ne'er allowed the Christian right
To put a Christian man in chains.

And as the light more clearly shone,
When word of life was multiplied,
She girded up her loins afresh;
She softened vigorous codes of war;
She smiled in dungeon prison cells;
She lifted woman from her thrall,
And gave to home domestic joys;
Provided hospitals for sick,
And almshouse for the suffering poor;
She sought the blind, the deaf, the weak,
And made provision for their needs.
She built her homes for troubled souls,
Whose fancies had their reason ruled,
Where broken threads of tangled thought
Might join and grow to strength again.
And while she gave celestial hopes,
She also proved an earthly friend;
An angel soothing human woe,
The strongest, purest, earth has seen.

And now when Slavery's ranks are formed,
And commerce, law, and social life,
The press and party, pen and school,
As captains in his columns march,
With gaudy banners floating high,
The question comes: "Shall Christian Church,
The voice of God to dying men,
Be found on the oppressor's side?"

O Church of Christ! thy robes were soiled.
When Samson dallied in the lap
Of wanton, he was shorn of strength.
Thy holy vessels captured were
And borne away to foreign lands,
And princes, captains, used the same
To drink their wine and praise their gods;
The oppressor used the Christian bonds
Of peace, forgiveness, fear of God,
To closer bind the captive ones.
And used the ministers of Christ,
With twisted texts of holy truth,
To rivet carefully the chains.

A remnant left in Israel's ranks
Did never to this Baal bow.
But when the strife was waxing hot,
And prophets hunted to their caves,
They often felt they were alone.

Gradation in their words were found,
From open, shameless, bold defense,
Through every shade of sentiment,
To meek, regretful, mild excuse.
Some Southern preachers boldly said:
To us it is divinely given
The life of Slavery to preserve.
This trust we must forever keep
For God, and truth, and human weal;

And as in this we faithful are,
So God will sure defend our cause.
   Thus prophets blinded taught the blind.

   And others said, The word of God
Allows the ownership of men;
And if men choose the right to claim
To buy or sell the captive ones,
Whoever dares condemn their course,
Is found denying holy truth.

   And many said, The civil law
Controls these questions of the slave.
   The Church should never interfere
Where'er the law asserts its claims.
   Had Daniel, in the ancient time,
Or Hebrew children, doomed to burn,
With all the martyrs for the right,
But heard this famous Christian truth,
They easy had escaped the fires.

   And others said, It may be wrong
To hold a fellow-man in chains,
But still the Church should never say
The wrong of slavery we forbid;
Hard words will only gender strife.
   The Church should ever kindly speak,
And preach the Gospel truth to all,
Hoping the providential time
Will come, when masters shall be free
From burdens they so long have borne.
   And thus with *tweedle dum and dee*,
Some seemed to think they honored God,
And sought the welfare of the slave.

   But while these words, so lachrymose,
You scarce would think that they could feel
Emotions but of pitying love
For all the erring sons of men;

But when they talked of radicals,
Disturbers, of the Church and State,
Their pent-up zeal burst forth in flame,
And maledictions dire they spoke;
Anathema maranatha
Seemed language pleasant to their lips,
For wicked abolitionists.

And others still did really see
Slaveholding was a monstrous crime.
Bishops, and presidents at large,
And doctors of some high degree,
Whose anxious care was to preserve
The folds in which their flocks were penned;
And when the sharp collisions came,
Threatening to rend the Christian Church,
Should any cast these torments out;
With these their fears outgrew their faith,
And they passed by the other side.

In southern portion of the land,
Where Slavery held defiant sway,
The Church surrendered to his rule
Without division or dissent.
In Northern States, reputed free,
The Church was wavering in the strife,
And many, while they feared the Lord,
They served the idols of the land.
The churches of collective form
Were torn asunder in the storm,
And congregations rent in twain,
Or struggled with convulsive pain.
While slavery sought to crush in shame,
Whoe'er refused to laud his name.

Thus, in the great terrific strife,
The organic Church did largely give
Power and dominion to the beast.

Yet still a remnant held the truth;
Else Sodom and Gomorrah's guilt
Had whelmed the whole in judgment fires.

So to the powers that fiercely fought,
Beneath the black aggressive flag,
Which sought to dominate these lands,
With pain we add the Christian Church;
Her snow-white banner stained with dark,
Her captains with their marshaled hosts,
Their ensigns nodding as they marched,
Keeping the time which Slavery blew.
While Freedom, facing still her foes
With fevered eye and pallid brow,
Bruised and bleeding, worn and torn,
Her sword unsheathed, the scabbard gone,
Was slowly crowded from the field.

O, Truth and Righteousness divine!
O burning Love and holy Zeal!
O Justice! with thy flaming sword,
Immortal flames that wait His voice,
Hast thou no part in this affray?
Shall Freedom here be stricken down,
While powers of God stand idly by?
But hush, my soul, why question so?
It is not thine His ways to judge.

VIII.

THE WOES AND CRIMES OF SLAVERY.

THE spirits of the hidden world,
  Invisible to mortal sight,
  Become incarnate on the earth;
They speak with fleshly human lips,
They strike and rend with human hands,
And lead men captive at their will.
  Oppression, spirit of the pit,
Possesses here a human form,
Producing ever woe and crime.
  Of these we would essay to speak.

  Within that monumental pile
Where England garners up her great,
Beneath Westminster's vaulted roof,
Among her kings and titled ones,
Historians, poets, and divines,
Whose works in letters, arts, and arms
Have been their country's ornament,
And glory for a thousand years,
A newly chiseled slab declares:
  "Beneath this stone in quiet rests
Remains of DAVID LIVINGSTONE,
Who, borne by loving, willing hands
O'er many a league of land and sea,
Was here committed to the dust."
  And who was David Livingstone,
To give him burial place so rare?
And what the motives of his work?

An humble minister of Him
Who came to save the lost; he went
To seek the lost in Africa.
  With loving gifts for leading men
He traveled o'er the inland plains,
He crossed the mountain heights unknown,
He traced the rivers to their source,
And then he traced them to the sea.
  With careful eye he still observed
The people, climate, soils, and fruits,
And thus he added to the store
Of useful knowledge of these lands.
  He followed many tortuous paths,
And threaded many pathless wilds,
For years continuing in this work.

  And while the world his work applauds,
It was incited and controlled
By reasons other than they knew;
His late recorded words declare:
  "My object is to find the source
And fountain of the trade in slaves;
I wish to live and help to heal
This open sore of all the world."

  This, then, the motive of the man,
To follow up the sinuous path
Of fetid stream unto its source;
To pour the balm of Christian truth
Upon the plague-spot of the race,
From whence its life was drained away.
  Heroic, noble, Christian man,
Thou'rt worthy of thy resting place.

  Within the heart of Africa,
Two thousand miles from ocean tides,
A stream meanders through the vale,
And drops into the placid lake;

While mountains stand as sentinels
Around the peaceful scene below.
  The remnant of a broken tribe,
Wasted by sanguinary war,
Had hither fled ; and, unpursued,
Had found a shelter in this vale.
  And years had passed, their huts were built,
Their fields were tilled, their cotton spun,
And from their fields, the lake, the wilds,
They gathered sustenance for their needs;
Protected by th' All-Father's care.

  But lands five thousand miles away,
Producing sugar, coffee, spice,
Were fallow; wanting willing hands.
  And thus a motive reached that vale
To bring those hands this work to do;
That idle men who held these lands
Might reap the harvests of their toil.

  The light was breaking in the east,
The birds were trilling matin song,
The bees were murmuring in the hives,
The morning wind disturbed the leaves
And roughed the waters of the lake,
As life was waking in the huts
Where slept the dwellers of the vale.
  When, hark! tumultuous crash of arms,
With beat of drum and shouts of men,
And fires leaping from the thatch.
  And sleeping ones awoke to find
Their village burning in their sight,
And circled round with murderous foes.
  An hour had passed; the helpless ones,
Aged and infant, slept in death;
The rest have fetters on their limbs.

  By repetition of such acts

There soon are gathered lengthy trains;
Their fetters locked to iron chains.
  Thus cavalcade is speedy formed
And started forward toward the coast.
  With broken homes now 'whelmed in fire,
And broken hearts, they pass away,
Guarded and driven by human fiends.
  And weary days pass o'er their heads,
And nights their frames unrested lie.
  The iron crushing through the skin,
Hunger and thirst their flesh consumes,
While fevers waste their little strength,
And death doth daily thin their ranks.
  But on and on, a thousand miles,
Weary and worn, foot-sore and faint,
They pass; until the town is reached
Where Christian trader comes to change
His gew-gaws for their captured souls.

  So many yards of calico,
So many beads, so many knives,
So much of powder and of ball,
So much of brandy and of rum,
The products of these Christian lands,
To be exchanged for living men.
  The trade is made, the goods are passed,
The captives, with their masters new,
Must meet another thousand miles
The deaths and dangers of the way.

  Bewildered, torpid, blind, and dumb,
The stupor stunning sense of ill,
They reach the margin of the sea,
Are halted in the barracoon,
And wait the coming of the ships
To bear them hence to distant lands.

  The slave-ship waits beside the shore;
Her boats are out, the signal given,

The prison doors are open thrown,
The captives guarded to the beach,
And to the ship are soon transferred;
Hustled and crowded 'neath the deck,
The middle passage to endure.
  These pirate rovers of the deep
In later times must strictly hide
All traces of the freight they bear.

  How much the mortal frame can bear
Of filth and vermin, lack of food,
Of close confinement, fetid air,
And still retain the soul in life;
This thought alone doth mitigate
The woes and horrors of their state.

  Depression from exhausting toil,
Endured in traveling to the sea,
Aroused remembrance of their homes,
To which awakening sense returns;
The dread homesickness of the heart,
Conjoined with horrors all around,
And apprehension of their doom,
All seize them with o'erwhelming force,
And all the powers of life give way.
  Thus every new return of morn
The crowded hold yields up her dead.
  With ribald jest, or bitter curse,
The dead are thrown into the sea.
  O, sea! thy secrets none can tell
Till earth and sea shall yield their dead.

  The horrors of the passage past,
Survivors stand upon the shore,
To factors in this trade consigned.
  Their orders show their patrons needs;
For male and female, old and young,
In twos and threes, in tens and scores,

For north and south, for home and field,
And speedy are these orders filled.
  The rest are in the auction mart,
And public sold at highest price.

  Where now are fathers and their sons?
Where mothers and their daughters dear?
Husband and wife, and early love?
  Scattered and torn like autumn leaves
Swept by the fierce tornado's blast.
  In Afric's jungles some are found,
And some beneath the ocean wave;
Some toil in rice and cotton fields,
And brood in silence o'er their wrongs;
And some, enraged and insolent,
Are whipped and kicked and starved and burned.
  And who alive, and who are dead,
Of friends to whom their hearts were joined,
None but the Infinite can know.

  Commerce may briefly be defined:
Exchange of those commodities
In excess found in any place
For the supply of others' need.
  It deals in products of the soil,
In coal and metals from the mines,
In varied work of artisan,
Whose touch transforms to beauteous use;
In horse and ox, for useful toil,
In beef and mutton, for our food;
And thus through distribution wide
The yields of each serve needs of all.

  The parent state of presidents
Added another branch of trade.
  The fancy farmers of the land
Oft meet in fairs and cattle shows
To note improvement of their stock.

And prices fabulous are paid
For sire or dam which shall eclipse
The best of other breeds or lands.
 Virginia and her compeer States
Turned their attention to produce—
Not fancy horse, nor mammoth ox—
They bred and sold their living men!

Upon the rolling broken land,
Between the mountains and the sea,
On tributary of Roanoke,
Virginia planter lived at ease.
Hundreds of acres in his lands,
And scores of slaves to till the same,
He raised tobacco, corn, and wheat,
He kept his carriage, drank his wine,
Attended church, and rode to town;
His friends from town their visits made,
And preachers met around his board;
And thus his days were passed away,
In honor and in opulence.
 With outward show of purity
He had his favorite female slaves,
And dark and white did strangely blend
In negro quarters on his place.

 Among the children growing there,
A boy his master's features took.
 The mother was of mingled blood;
Her olive cheek and languid eye,
With rounded form and active grace,
Had brought her beauty's fatal dower,
And youthful mother she became;
Her boy's complexion bright and fair;
While favors such as slaves may know
He had while he to manhood grew.

 The wife of this Virginia lord,
Was from a Richmond city home;

Her family for many years
Subsisting on the toil of slaves;
By birth and training thus prepared
To put unpleasant things away
From sight and thought, and live at ease.

   From time to time a brother came
To visit at his sister's home.
   Here, free from fashion's gilded chains,
Without domestic bonds or cares,
He often spent the summer weeks.
   Passion was strong, and conscience weak,
Virtue with him was but a name;
His blood was mingled in the veins
Of one whose mother was in bonds;
His daughter was without his name.

   This girl in early life was brought
From Negro quarters to the house.
   Alert and active in her step,
With eye for order, tidy hand,
As years gave vigor to her frame,
She was installed the chamber-maid;
And here so well her work was done,
She won the place of waiting-maid,
The highest place that servants found.

   And now, with dress and ornament
Becoming to the place she filled,
When friends, of wealth and station came
To while away the summer hours,
Or ladies traveled, as was style,
To Sulphur Springs, or Hanging Bridge,
The Saratogas of the South,
Or spent the season in the town
Among the Richmond dames and lords;
The waiting-maid must ever be
A noted portion of the train.

And pride and vanity conspired
To show her beauty and her grace;
That envious ones might be apprised
What lofty style was thus attained
Attended by such service rare.

And though deprived of schools and books,
And standing in a menial's place,
Her soul drank in surrounding light
As buds absorb the morning dews;
And forms of beauty, music's art,
Met answering voices in her soul,
Responsive to their lightest touch
Her mingled blood in vigor ran,
Freshening the bloom upon her cheek
And giving sparkle to the eye.
In place and gifts so much preferred,
She seemed to 'scape the bitter curse
That rests upon the lowly born.

While she thus passed life's op'ning years,
The youth, who bore Caucasian look
Tinged with that mellowed olive shade
Received from her whose name he bore,
Had also changed from boy to man.
His master's favor had upborne
In part the weight which on him lay.
He was a leader on the farm,
He oft was driver to the town,
And sometimes brought the needed wares
On orders from the master's hand.

Love's mystic spell fell on those hearts;
Joined in a common lowly lot,
By others' sins first joined in shame,
Mingling the blood from wide-spread zones,
Quickened by force from dominant race
And by surrounding circumstance,

Together drawn toward higher state;
When passion wakened in their souls,
Not strange that Cupid's arrows fell
And wounded both their hearts alike.

The crowning human bliss is love,
That love which meets with full return;
It swallows every other sense
And fills and permeates the soul.
'Tis fed with flashes of the eye,
With snatch of song and whispered words,
With dainty touch of finger tips.
And cultured souls, whose wider range
Traverses richer lores of earth,
When passion strikes these mystic keys,
Then thrill with chords and harmonies,
Rich, sweet, and full, beyond compare.

The being filled with these delights
Sees beauty in the plainest face.
As burning lamp within the vase
Changes the clay to shining pearl,
So brightness shines from every brow
Illumed and glorified by love.

Thus these two hearts, whose humble state
Debarred the great pursuits of earth,
Found sweetest solace in their love,
A love acknowledged, each to each,
A love encouraged in the house,
A love the master ne'er forbade.
What bliss then filled each passing hour,
The sunlight never shone so bright;
All labor was performed with ease;
And when the mistress granted leave
To spend together evening hours,
'T was almost like the golden gates
Which open for earth's wearied souls.

And thus they spent the passing months,
Waiting some happy Christmas time
To celebrate their wedding day.

Another joy to these was given,
A hope scarce less than hopes of heaven.
A change had in the master grown,
The fires of youthful passion cooled,
The long-hushed voice within was heard
Calling toward higher, better life.
A retrospection of the past
Showed many blots upon the page,
And empty spaces, still unfilled
With noble, worthy, Christian deeds.

Survey of present scenes revealed
The active days of life now past;
The eye waxed dim, the cunning hand
Losing the deftness of its touch;
The silver shining in the hair,
Tokens of coming wintry life.
A burden rested on his soul;
A sense of guilt still unforgiven,
A fear of coming, future ills.
Thus pressed, he turned to Christian truth,
He sought in prayer for light divine,
Resolved the better life to lead.
As Christian light more clearly shone,
He saw environments around
Which seemed impossible to break.

When weeks of anxious thought had passed,
A well-formed purpose filled his soul.
The boy, to whom his heart was warm,
Fruit of his early sinful ways,
Should have this gift: he should be free.

Returning from the town one day,

Seated together side by side
The master and his slave were found.
  In silence, with abstracted air
And puzzled look, the master rode;
His lips had moved as if in prayer,
The tears were starting in his eyes,
When, turning to the boy, he spoke:
"How would you like it to be free?"

  An angel, standing in his path,
With kingly robes to clothe his form,
And golden crown to deck his brow,
Would not have given more surprise.
  A flash of joy o'erspread his face
Like sunshine from a stormy sky;
And then the blood forsook his cheek,
Rushing upon the font of life,
While every member of his frame
Quivered and trembled with the weight
Of hopes now struggling to the birth.

  Awhile he found his voice to say:
Master was always very kind,
But master knew the best for him;
If master thought he might be free,
He would be very, very glad.

  And then the master spoke again
With measured words, affecting calm.
  The boys at home could work the place;
He soon could learn to work a farm,
And be the master for himself.
  His son from college would return,
And he could share the master's care.
  The master knew he loved the girl,
And she should also be made free.
  He would buy them a pleasant home
Up in the North, where all were free.

And master, he would sometimes come,
To see him growing rich and great.

These little words so kindly spoke,
Freight with such precious, priceless store,
Spoken as to a brother man,
They fell upon that bursting heart
As waters cool the burning lips,
Or pardon comes beneath the rope.
 The tears were streaming from his eyes,
Convulsive sobs swept through his frame,
Making an agony of joy.

The good he never dared to hope
Was laid so freely at his feet;
He would be free—no more a slave;
A man, and stand with men upright,
Have wife and home forever sure,
And all the blessings freedom brings.
 His soul was stirred to deepest depth,
The streams of bliss o'erflowed their banks,
And deluged all the powers of life.

When subsidence of joy took place,
And he could look in face of him
Who had bestowed these blessed gifts,
But small return of words was made.
 The light now shining from the eyes,
The flush that overspread his face,
More plainly told than human words
How great the boon he had received.

The master's plans were clearly told,
After the son should have returned,
And be acquainted with the work.
 His wedding-day should early come;
And then the newly married pair
To their new home should be removed.

But boys at home must never know
What master was to do for him.
　Some must remain to work the farm,
And they could not protect themselves.
　He should go on as in the past,
Should lead the farm and do the work,
Till all was ready for the change.

　Did e'er the shining stars behold
Two happier souls than those who walked,
Upon a balmy summer eve,
Beneath the blooming orchard trees,
Talking of that expected home
Whose fields and groves, whose fruit and flowers,
Should be a paradise restored.

　They had received the new white stone,
With name engraved no other knows;
And day by day they gazed within
The shining symbols there to see,
Which, blazing with celestial light,
Forever read, " I shall be free."

　The summer solstice quickly passed,
And cooler autumn days had come.
　The college son was now at home,
Wearing his *alma mater's* crown.
　Harvests were gathered from the fields,
And vine and tree had shed their store.
　The nuts were dripping in the woods,
And jasper, golden, crimson hues,
Were mingled in the forest robes.
　Earth was preparing for her rest,
Disrobing from work-day attire,
She donned to wear, an evening hour,
The figured robe, th' embroidered shoe,
Before she lay her wearied limbs
Beneath the down from northern seas.

The sons of toil in southern lands
Were looking to the Christmas time,
When rest from work, and clothing new,
With visits, gifts, and feast, and song
Should sunshine shed o'er troubled ways.
   And some beyond this golden beam
Were looking to a brighter morn,
When every cloud should pass away;
And sun should never more go down.
   For in that hoped-for nothern land,
It seemed no night could ever come.

   The bright October morning sun
Was mounting upward in the sky,
When sire and son—the lawful heir—
Were sitting by the father's desk,
Speaking of various future plans,
Of house and lands, of crops and gains,
Which it was well the son should know.
   The coals were glowing in the grate,
Tempering the air to pleasant warmth.
   The well-swept room, the maps and books,
The flowers blooming near the light,
The manly forms of age and youth,
A cheerful pleasant picture made.

   With hesitating air the sire,
Some papers from his drawers took;
Said he, "These papers are the deeds
Of freedom for the boy and girl,"
Giving the names the son well knew,
"Which I design this day to take
And have recorded in the court."
   It cost an effort thus to speak,
Suggesting thoughts which ne'er had words
Between the father and the son.
   The deep emotions of his soul
Were shaking both his hand and voice.

The son, by many passions moved,
Some which the future may reveal,
And some, oppression's common fruit,
The father's words had filled with rage.
  In tones of bitter scorn he cried:
"Niggers were only fit for slaves,
And lowest, meanest, worst of all,
Were the white niggers on the place."

  Unto the father words like these
Were like a goad that pierced the skin,
Or burning fire on naked flesh.
  They touched the sorest spot of all,
And stung and roused him like a blow.
  His face was livid in his rage,
While every member of his frame
Quivered and struggled, held in leash
By effort of a giant will.
  This for a moment, lo! a groan,
And then a crash, a prostrate form.
  The tension had been too severe,
The cord had snapped, the bowl was broke,
The moving wheels would only turn
Until the cistern spent its force.
  His work was done for good or ill,
And life was oozing slow away.
  The help was called, the master laid
Upon his bed, no more to rise.
  Under the keys were safely placed
The papers fallen from his hands.

  As gallant vessel, stanch and trim,
Moved by its own internal fires,
Cutting its way through placid seas,
Under the blaze of midday sun,
With vitals torn by hidden rock,
A moment struggles with the shock,
Careens, and settles in the deep,

With all its freight of priceless souls,
So every human joy and hope,
Bound up within that mortal life,
With him went down into the depths.

That fatal day had slowly passed,
The neighbors hastened to the house,
Physicians came and tried their arts,
And turned away without a hope.
The lowly ones came in to gaze
Upon their dying master's face,
And make their moans and shed their tears,
His wife was borne convulsed away.
The watchers waited by the bed
With voices hushed. The stert'rous breath
Grew fainter as the hours advanced.

The son sat by the father's desk,
And took the papers from their place.
He looked upon the even lines,
Traced by his father's steady hand;
The room was clear, the curtains drawn,
The fire still burning in the grate;
He thrust the papers in the coals,
And saw them shrivel in the blaze.
Could others looked, they might have seen
Their golden hopes to ashes turn.

The course of time ne'er stops his way
For human griefs, or pain, or death.
The human bubbles form and burst,
And others follow in their course.
The sun shines on, and people live,
With all the brightness gone from life.

The bondman once his brother asked
Of promises the father made.
Reply was made, of nigger lies,

And vengeful threats, should e'er he dare
To speak of such a subject more.
   And she to whom his faith was pledged,
With modest, shrinking, trembling fear,
Made sad report of threatened shame,
Thus vainly seeking needed aid
From him who had no power to save.
   The slave one day a meeting sought
With her to whom his soul was bound—
He had a plan for their escape.
   The master, coming from his ride,
The servant saw within the house,
And sternly ordered him away.
   When their eyes met, the master saw
A blaze of fury burning there,
Which seemed to say, a little more,
Nor man, nor God, nor heaven, nor hell,
Should stay his hand, but he would tear
The heart from him who had destroyed
The bliss and glory of his life.

   A notice in the weekly sheet
Said able-bodied, youthful hands
Were wanted for the *Texas* trade.
   The following day the carriage went,
Bearing the master to the town.
   The place was reached, the bargain struck
With purchaser of human souls.
   The carriage ordered to the door,
The master entered with a friend,
Giving directions where to drive.
   Arrived, the slave was sent within,
A parcel from his friend to bring.
   The door was entered, key was turned,
The master drove the team away.

   The book divine doth sometimes tell
Of joy unspeakable and full

Of glory. And if human words
Are insufficient to declare
The possibilities of joy
With which the soul of man is thrilled,
Much less can words, or tears, or groans
Unload the weight of agony
Compressed and borne by stricken ones.

Had stones been those of Palestine,
Habakkuk heard from out the wall,
Crying against oppression dire;
Or stones in Salem's streets of old,
Waiting to cry to own their Lord;
Or were there power in sighs of slaves,
Like songs and prayers apostles spoke,
Those prison walls were shrieks and groans,
And earthquake powers had plowed its depths.

But all is still; the soul alone
Goes out from God and light and life,
Goes to the coffle-gang and chain,
Goes to the *Texas* cotton fields,
Goes to the lash, the branding fire,
To mingle memories of love
And hopes, now dead of earthly joy,
With torments such as fill the soul
Where hate, revenge, and fury reign;
To pass in pain the fleeting years,
And then sink down, unwept, to death.

Or shall our words attempt to tell
Her fate, bereft of only friend?
Can virtue stand against the shock,
Where power and passion join to crush?
The scenes of former years return;
And when the bloom of youth is past,
A sale to *Georgia's* cotton fields
Removes from sight of him, who crushed
A human soul, his finished work.

When birds of prey are on the wing,
Affrighted fowls for shelter seek.
When hungry wolves invade the flock,
Then fright and wounds and death abound.
Tornadoes sweep o'er forests wide,
And leave destruction in their path;
Or moving through the peopled lands,
Cities and towns in ruins fall.
The cyclone, whirling o'er the sea,
Scatters the wrecks along the shore.
At the destroying angel's touch
The dead are left in every house.

But none of these more terror bring
Than negro trader, when he comes
To tear away the lowly ones
For sale in Slavery's southern marts.
As tigers' presence near the fields
Carries dismay to flocks and herds,
Which, dumb with terror, flee for help
To man, or hide in jungle deep,
So human flocks in terror shrink
When human prowlers seek their prey,
But have no help in man to gain,
And dare not hide from sight away.

The dread alarm from lip to lip
Is whispered through the threatened flocks.
The fears and apprehensions dire
With trembling weakness fills the frame,
And chills the marrow in the bones.
From time to time a stealthy glance
Anticipates the dreadful call;
And when the hopeless summons comes,
The hoe drops from his nerveless hands,
The blood forsakes his ebon cheek,
And looking not to right or left,
No outstretched hand, no farewell word,

He parts from all in life held dear;
Sold to the doom he ever shrank,
From whence time never brings return.

A father and a husband he,
His wife and children still remained
The chattels that another owned.
  She daily wrought to till his fields,
And coin her sweat into his gold;
Or else she tastes the bitter pain
Of motherhood, to swell his gains.
  The Sabbath past, awhile he stayed
Within the cabin where she dwelt,
And ate with her the food she earned.
  His children sat upon his knee,
Their twining arms around his neck,
Their velvet cheeks against his lips,
The mother looking on with joy.
  He left such tokens of his love
As slaves in penury can give,
With promise of a soon return.

  But all is past. His heart beats on,
But he is dead to those he loved,
And wife and children dead to him;
A lingering, anguished, living death.

  Another place a boy was bought,
Some fifteen summers he had seen.
  His mother in her early days
Had never known a parent's love.
  To satisfy a sheriff's claim
Sold, and removed from all she knew.
  The youthful father of her child
In spring-time of his life had died,
And all the fountains of her love
Were poured upon her darling boy.
  His infant beauty was her joy,

His growing strength her boast and pride;
The passing summers swiftly wrought
To mold and tint his ripening powers.
　His youthful beauty, active grace,
His ready feet and willing hands,
His locks of jet, and teeth of pearl;
The proud and happy mother felt
No treasure like her loving boy.

　A merchant prince of *New Orleans*,
Whose marble mansion, fountains, grounds,
Provoked the envy of the mass,
Had asked the trader for a boy
To match the beauty of the place.

　The trader, watching for his prey,
As sharks for careless bathers wait,
Saw pass the mother and her child,
Laughing and chatting as they went.
　As hawk swoops down on chicken yard,
He came and tore the child away.
　Her heart was broke, her all was lost;
The boy was added to the train.

　And thus by ones and twos and threes
The train was slowly gathered up.
　Sometimes a maid, whose lover's kiss
But yesternight was on her lips.
　Sometimes a mother, with her babe,
Leaving the husband of her choice,
And children of an earlier birth ;
The fairer ones of mingled blood,
Bought to supply a base demand;
The freedom-loving ones, who sought
Escape from their dark prison house;
The brutal, coarse, and insolent,
Whom whips or torture could not tame;
The dark and white, the old and young,

Some breathing forth the words of prayer,
And some with curses on their lips,
Their wrists locked in a common chain:
They pass away from all they loved,
The gates of darkness round them close,
Which shall be opened nevermore.

The soldiers of imperial Rome,
Returning from successful war,
Laden with spoils from conquered realms,
At first the custom introduced
Of auction sale. They thus disposed
The trophies pillaged from their foes.
The barbed spear thrust in the ground
Was made the symbol of their work.

The auction's rise, and symbols show
The adaptation in its use
To merchandise of living men.
For men were pillaged of their rights,
By conqueror's power were overborne,
And captives held as spoils for sale.
The spears are thrust in throbbing hearts,
Whose barbs can never be withdrawn
Till cords of life are cut in twain.

The rapid change from youth to age,
From silken cords to iron bands,
In nothing else is plainer seen
Than phases of the specter, Debt.
'Tis Credit, Trust, and pleasant words,
The glowing picture all is fair
Until the bond is written out.
The pleasant features soon depart,
And Debt, hard visaged, now must give
The pound of flesh writ in the bond;
And Shylocks of the present time,
Their bonds will take the blood and bone.

The judgment shuts its iron grip,
And chattels are announced for sale.

A motley throng is soon convened,
The profit and the sport to share.
The broken, refuse, worthless wares
Are offered first, to please the mass
With little money in their purse.
And some there are great bargains get
In cast-off cart or broken plow,
In ancient loom, or spinning-wheel;
And while the salesman cries these things
He takes the measure of the crowd.
Then follow horses, cattle, sheep,
The blooded bays, the carriage fine,
The costly furnish of the house,
Carpets and mirrors, pictures rare,
The table service, rich and full,
The choice piano—Steinway grand,
All pass the salesman's flippant tongue
As grass is dropped before the scythe.

While these events were passing by,
The wines and liquors, freely drank,
Had loosed the tongues of thoughtless ones,
And impious oath or ribald jest
Their coarse and vulgar grade revealed,
While reckless disregard of price
Gave token of the wine-cup's powers.
The way now being full prepared,
The "people" were set up for sale.

The first one called was known as "George;"
Some threescore summers had he seen,
And faithful labor through these years
Had seamed his face and bowed his frame.
With him had come life's evening hour,
When many seek relief from toil.

The farmer lays aside his plow,
The merchant closes oft his trade,
To eat the bread his hands had earned
During his earlier, active years.
 And George, whose life had ne'er known rest,
He now had prospect of a change.
 But not the vine-embowered cot,
Or modest mansion 'neath the trees,
Mid orchard fruits and flowers' bloom,
The future mirrored in his sight.

 But, "Stand up, George, hold up your head,
And look the buyers in the face;
None of your baby sniveling now.
 There, gentlemen, behold a boy,
An honest, faithful, willing boy.
 His woman's dead, his children gone,
He never goes to see his wife,
He never tries to run away,
And will not shirk his daily work.
 He's tough and hardy, as you see;
How much is bid for such a man?"

 And then they gather round the man;
They feel the muscles of his arms,
They note the labor-calloused hands,
The bent and stiffened finger joints,
They search his back, his hips, his limbs,
For marks of whip or iron brand;
They thrust their fingers in his mouth,
To note condition of his teeth;
While auctioneer doth glibly talk
Of all his truthful, pious ways,
To which the crowd pays little heed.

 Insurance science closely weighs
The probabilities of life;
And rates its risks from tables made
Of many lives, through lengthened years.

The science which these bidders have
Was never written in a book.
Its tabulated forms would show
The griefs, the pains, the loneliness,
Contempt, derision, and disdain,
Which dry the juices of the soul,
Destroy the vigor of the will,
And leave the wheels of life to grind
Without their lubricating oil.

These ask alone: "How much of toil
The failing mortal frame can bear,
Before the soul shall break away
From earthly thrall forever free?"
So much of gold for human brain,
For flesh and sinew, blood and bone,
So much for breath divine of lives,
Erst breathed into the new-formed clay;
So much for Christ, who meekly stands
In person of his suffering one,
And takes the gibes, the taunt, the scorn,
As done unto himself alone.

The bids are made from side to side;
Slower and slower mounts the price,
Until it stops. The last who speaks
Has never owned a foot of land,
Or other valued earthly thing;
A coarse, ill-natured, brutal man.
A little money, to him left,
The product of a brother's toil,
He pays, that he may own a slave.
And George is "going," "going," "gone,"
To such a master in his age.

The next, "A lively wench," he said,
"Not quite so handsome now as once,
But still she's strong, and spry to work,

Can 'tend the children, sweep the house,
Or pick the cotton, hoe the corn;
Her name is Moll. How much for her?"

A woman, shriveled, bent, and gray,
Whose fiery spirit all her years
Had chafed and worn the strings of life,
Making her old before her time,
Now stood upon the auction block.
Husband and children of her youth
Were either dead or lost from sight;
She had a "man" on neighboring farm,
But seldom did she see his face.
A buyer for the cotton-fields
Noted her fingers, long and thin,
The supple motions of her limbs;
He thought her life might last two years.
His bids advanced beyond the rest,
And quickly she was struck to him.
Some families were also sold,
Husband and wife and little ones.
When bids were free, they went in bulk;
When buyers asked, each by themselves;
While every one was strictly watched,
Defects and virtues close observed,
And youth and beauty, female charms,
Habits and health, and manly strength,
They each were rated at a price.

The story of each humble life,
Its hopes and fears, its joys and pains,
While all, which was to them the world,
Broke and dissolved before their view,
Is only written in the books,
To be revealed when men are judged.

Among the last, that day of doom,
There came a mother and her boy.

She was a servant of the house;
She knew the kitchen's mysteries all,
And well was versed in household ways.
   The best of bread and cakes and pies,
Puddings and tarts, and savory stews,
Came deftly from her willing hands;
And in the bills which told the sale,
A first-class cook she was declared.
   Her boy had seen some twenty months,
Healthy and beautiful and bright,
His baby laugh and lisping words
Were music in his mother's ear.
   Her eye was on him in her work,
She slept, his arms about her neck.

   The mistress of the house, who taught
The servant all her useful ways,
When ruin stared them in the face,
With loss of all their pleasant things,
A promise made, to intercede,
To keep the mother with the child,
When dreaded day of sale should come.

   The servant felt, 'twas sad indeed,
To see the beauteous house laid waste,
Which sheltered all they so much loved;
But mistress, while she lost her home,
No one could take her child away,
While could she only keep her boy,
The storm would lose its greatest force.
   When called to stand on auction block,
She took her baby in her arms.

   A voice among the crowd cried out,
"Put down the child, let each be sold
Only to those who wish to buy."
   The mother looked from side to side,

A maniac wildness in her eye,
And closer grasped her frightened boy.
"Give me the child," said auctioneer,
Pulling to take the boy away,
While coarse and vulgar oaths were heard,
Mingling their cadence with his screams.

The mistress heard the cry and ran,
Her head uncovered, to the scene.
With voice by tears and anger choked
She cried: "For shame! leave her the boy."
And others cried, "For shame!" "For shame!"
And so the mother and her child
Were offered to the waiting crowd.
Some moved by pity, some by greed,
The bids came rapid, sharp, and strong,
Till far above the usual price.

The voice that cried, "Put down the child,"
Was from a city man afar,
The keeper of a grand hotel.
An extra cook he wished to find,
And after due inquiry made,
Was certain what he sought was found.
But cooks and waiters must not have
Children for whom they need to care;
So when the mother and her child
Were standing on the block for sale,
He only wished the first to buy.

But when the two were sold at once,
His bids kept pace with others there,
Till hundreds, seven, eight, and nine,
And tens, and fives, were added still,
And "Going, going," cried the voice,
"One thousand dollars, going, gone,
To Mr. Grinder, from the town;"
Mother and boy to him are sold.

The work was drawing to a close;
The sheriff making bills of sale,
The check of Grinder certified
Was taken in, the papers passed,
All things were done in legal form,
And Grinder owned the persons bought.
　Then turning to his new-bought slave,
"We start for home to-night," he said;
"Be ready in one hour from now."

　With mistress' help, she gathered soon
The little that she called her own,
With clothing for her darling one.
　Trembling, she passed from room to room,
The boy close clinging to her neck.
　While this had passed within, without
Another sale was quickly made;
A buyer, there, his business was
The raising slaves for southern trade;
To him had Grinder sold the boy.

　The carriage stood before the door,
And Jane was called to get within.
　"Give me the boy," the master said,
Tearing him from her sheltering arms.
　The air was filled with shrieks and screams,
As carriage wheels rolled swift away.
　Death does not come to those who wish,
Else she had been no more a slave.
　And thus these lowly ones were torn
And scattered from their former home.

　And often scenes like these occurred,
Without improvidence or debt.
　The lordly planter of the South,
Thousands of acres his estate,
Worked by his many hundred slaves,
Was not an ogre of his kind.

The toil of many able hands
With golden stores his coffers filled.
His sons were trained in college halls,
And merchants, doctors, statesmen made.
His daughters, polished and refined,
The wives of cultured men became.
One was a city pastor's wife.
And one became the leading star,
Of social circle, which revolved,
Around White House at *Washington.*

The toil of black and calloused hands
Had polished all these jewels rare,
And while the planter held the reins,
God's rain and sunshine freely given,
With virgin wealth of fertile soil,
These toiling ones did fast transmute
To gold and other valued things.

But Death, who walks with equal force
Through cottage and through palace gates,
The threshold of this mansion passed,
His chilling breath was on the air,
And wheels of life, which seventy years
Had run, without a moment's rest,
Were stopped at once. The eyes were closed,
The hand was limp, the heart was still.

When proper time had intervened,
The persons having legal charge
Distributed the vast estate.

For days the public sale went on;
Like city swept by conquering fire
From house to house, from street to street,
Consuming in its onward course,
Temple and palace, hall and hut,
Which leaves naught scatheless in its path;

So each and all of the vast throng
Of lab'ring, suff'ring, helpless ones,
Stood trembling on the auction block.
  They saw the greedy vulture face
Of hungry crowd, mad to devour;
Which seethed and roared like raging flame,
Consuming every social tie,
Leaving, in place of humble joys,
But desolation, pain, and woe.

  The sale complete, executors
Allotted each their portion due.
  It added to the merchant's stock,
And built a warehouse for his use.
  The doctor built a larger house
Among the nabobs of the town;
He put the rest away in stocks.
  The politician took his share,
To pave ambition's rugged road,
Hoping when winning place of power,
Repayment from the public purse.
  The city pastor's polished wife,
Her house and person, plenished new,
Shining among the proudest there,
While rents and profits in his thoughts
Mingled with ministries of grace.
  The brilliant wife of senator,
Surprise and envy stirred anew,
With gold and pearls and diamonds rare,
Of highest price and richest hue.

  And thus the world went bravely on,
And all forgot, or thus they seemed,
That cries of those who reaped their fields,
The Lord of Sabaoth's ears had 'reached,
And cankered gold, from crime and wrong,
Would eat their flesh as it were fire.

The triumphs of inventive art
Have multiplied the powers of man,
A thousand-fold in many fields.
  But Nature moves with even step,
Unawed by Steam's majestic power,
Nor hastened by his whirling wheels.
  And forms of labor, nearest earth,
Where she unfolds her secret ways,
The more demand the thinking mind
And human hand to share her work.
  Machinery cannot hoe the corn,
Nor pick the cotton in the field.

  Behold a ripening cotton field;
A hundred acres it contains,
Stretching o'er hill-side, mount, and vale;
Its blended colors, dark and white,
Bowing before the summer winds,
Where sea of green is fringed with foam,
Like ocean billows rocked by storm.

  The crisis of the year is here,
The planting, weeding, watering past;
The value of these days of toil
Has culminated in this bloom.
  If gathered now, it profit brings,
Neglected, soon the storms will come,
And broken, drenched, and crushed to earth,
The hoped-for gains will all depart.
  But Slavery knows no spur of gain,
No fear of loss from coming storm.
  No gain augments the weekly dole,
Of pound of meat or peck of corn.
  The motives man applies to man
Are not for slaves, but, like the beasts,
They're driven only by the lash.

  In northern climes, where men are free,

The varied industries are found
Adapted to the tastes of each.
 And some prefer to till the soil,
While some pursue mechanic arts,
Some dig the ways for iron roads,
For public weal some merchants are,
While learned professions some employ.
 And thus in school, in church, in court,
In mines, in ships, in shop and farm,
They all contribute to the store
Of public good and private need.

 But some too lazy were to work,
Too proud to beg, too dull to learn,
And cowards, therefore, dare not steal.
 They took on earth the lowest place,
Became slave-drivers for the South.

 Before the break of morning light,
The horn resounded through the huts,
Bidding the weary ones prepare
For toil and pain another day.
 The morning meal was quickly eat—
'Twas only meal in haste prepared.
 And when the light o'er eastern hills
Was streaming through the gates of morn,
And bird and beast and leaf and flower
Rejoiced to greet the new-made day,
These toiling ones, with food and sleep
But half sufficient for their need,
Crowded and jostled in the path,
Like beasts are driven to the field,
The baskets carried for their work,
With which to bring appointed pounds.

 Under this system falsehood thrives,
And plans are laid to shirk their task;
While real sickness, when it came,
And head was filled with throbbing pain,

With fever coursing through the veins,
Was treated as a lying sham.
　Like patient horse, that ne'er complains
Till dropping down before his load,
So these are driven by the lash,
Complaints unheard, or heeded not,
Till Nature's powers are wholly spent.
　The soldier, serving in the field,
From duty always is excused
When sickness seizes him for prey.
　The driver's diagnosis is,
The lash applied with furious rage:
By this he tests the subject's health.

　The old are there, with whitened locks,
With bowing forms and trembling limbs.
　The child is there, whose tender years
Demand the forces of his life
To build and nourish growing frame.
　The recent mother, with her babe,
Now laid beneath a sheltering bush,
Wearied and worn she strives to work,
And also from her fevered blood
Supply the food her babe demands.
　Feeble and strong, the coarse and vile,
The innocent and pure alike,
All are compelled their place to take,
From break of morn to setting sun,
The fleecy fiber to secure.

　Through all that day of burning toil,
The driver walked from side to side,—
His head was sheltered from the blaze,—
Watching their motions as they worked,
Using his whip from time to time
When any lingered at their task,
And marking, in his angry moods,
Some to be whipped when work was done.

Meanwhile the day is hastening on,
And sun is sinking in the west.
Two visions break on human sight,
Unlike as those the gulf divides
Where Lazarus and the rich man dwell.

The glorious beauty of the sky,
Where heavenly limner spreads his field.
With pencil braided of the light,
On background of ethereal blue,
He overlays the evening cloud,
And then with rapid, silent touch,
Throws out the grand majestic lines.
Then pencil moves, and richest hues,
Of scarlet, purple, crimson, gold,
Are interlaced with fold on fold,
Revealing visions Patmos saw;
A mingled sea of glass and fire.
Thus curtained by this glorious scene,
And folding slow his gorgeous train,
The king of day withdraws from sight.
Then one by one the silent stars
Break through the curtains of the light,
Till flames the glory of the night.

These transformations of the sky,
Kaleidoscope of closing day,
Were mirrored on the earth beneath.
Her mountain tops were crowned with gold,
While darkness, from lethean founts,
Flowed slowly through the vales below,
And rising upward from the depths,
Enveloped forest, lake, and plain,
Till mountain tops were hid from sight,
And earth was mantled with the night.
Strange dissonance of Nature's march
With ever-varying harmonies,
And discords of the human soul.

The train is coming from the fields,
The fleecy burden piled on high,
And borne aloft, by unconquered will,
Or feebly dragging at their side.
Some earlier came with baskets filled,
But most had toiled till thick'ning night
Had mingled white and green in gray.
Their heavier motion, stiffened joints,
The faded sense of sight and touch,
More slowly piled the snowy mound;
And when the shadows closed the day,
With fears like those whose day of life
Has closed, with life's great work undone,
They started for the judgment-seat.

The crowd were gathered at the door
Waiting for sentence on their work.
Sufficient weight brought no response
Of cheering smile or pleasant word,
While those who failed met threat'ning words,
Should morrow's labor fail to add,
Recorded pounds deficient now.

This ordeal passed, their homes they seek;
No shining light from window-pane,
No sound of cheerful voice within,
No well-swept hearth greets their approach,
No song of kettle o'er the fire,
Nor savory fragrance of their food;
But darkness, filth, and blackened walls,
And couch of rags and fetid air,
Where morning winds and noonday sun
Have wrought no cleansing healthful power.

The fires kindled on the hearth,
The meal and water baked in haste,
And ate in weariness and pain;
The remnants waiting for the morn,

They seek their ill-kept resting place,
And in oblivion find relief.

   The ocean tides, whose ebb and flow,
Repeated are from day to day,
Give change and zest to every shore.
   They bathe afresh the sandy beach,
They sweep across the wide morass,
They enter in the coves and bays,
Mingling the saltness of the sea
With water from the mountain streams.
   Their currents pass the jutting rocks,
Which break their silver sheen to foam.
   They rock the vessels at the wharves,
Lifting their mammoth hulks aloft.
   They bathe the city's feet from stain,
And wash from every opening duct
The exhalations of her life,
And thence, in their returning flow,
They onward bear to open sea,
Corruptions which, uncleansed away,
Would poison all the springs of life;
And thus their ceaseless rise and fall,
Freshness and health give sea and land.

   But ocean has its stormy moods,
When waves in fury lash the beach,
And beat the rocks with angry roar,
When winds are loosed from all their caves,
And bellowing thunders join the fray.
   Then ocean, in her frantic wrath,
Dashes her ships on rocky coasts,
And wrecks whole navies in an hour.
   So great the change from sleeping seas,
And tides returning day by day,
To furious sweeping maddened might.

   So life its alternations hath,

Through all its ranks. From throned and
    crowned
To those who beg their daily bread,
And live in squalor, rags, and cold.
    Sometimes the tides of life flow smooth;
Anon the soul is filled with storms,
Which pour their fierce, resistless force,
Crushing whate'er withstands their way.

    And those, the slavery-burdened ones,
Whose daily lot to other eyes
Seemed full of bitterness and woe,
Were often called, through freak or fault,
To drink more bitter draughts of pain.

    Amid that crushed and burdened throng,
Who brought the product of their toil,
And gave account from day to day,
Before this human judgment-seat,
There walked one man with head unbowed.
    In stature, like the ancient Saul,
Above the common height of men.
    His chest was wide and deep and full,
And every member of his frame,
Compact and sinewy and strong,
His head well poised upon his neck,
His step was even, bold, and firm,
And e'en his naked feet had grace.
    The blood of Afric's untamed kings
Was shining in his lustrous eyes,
And archives of the torrid heats
Were found among his clust'ring curls,
While forehead broad and clear and high
Gave tokens of the thought and power
That flowed through his ancestral line.

    His youth was passed with small restraint,
And when he had to manhood grown,

Like full-grown colt, was hard to break;
When roused, with bit between his teeth,
His rider lost controlling power;
And so he passed from hand to hand
Till found in *Georgia's* cotton fields.

The unbent form, the undropped eye,
The step and carriage of a man,
Contained rebuke; was held menace
Toward him who sought, by threat and lash,
To make all bow where he held sway.

An aged man, whose whitened wool
And bowéd form proclaimed the years
Employed in unrequited toil,
His work presents. The scales were poised,
The scanty pile was wanting found.
When pride and avarice were the weights,
With which to balance eighty years
Of weakness, pain, and palsied limbs,
Not strange such weights were heaviest found.
Then oaths and imprecations dire
Were showered on his hoary head;
And to enforce these bitter threats,
The whip in angry mood was raised.

The Afric prince stood waiting there,
To age and weakness giving place.
These taunts, in him aroused a sense
Which philosophic Christian men
Among the virtues rank. A sense
Of pity for the suffering one,
Resentment for the wrong imposed.

He ne'er had studied in the books
To note the line where some divide,
Resentment for a flagrant wrong
From vengeance, which to God belongs.

The fire was flashing from his eye,
His muscles grew like cords of wire.
The driver, looking in his eyes,
Beheld the fury blazing there.
The whip, uplifted in his threat,
Toward the aged, trembling one,
Now fell with fierce, impulsive stroke,
Upon the face and o'er the eyes
Which blazed defiance of his power.

The braided strands of flaxen wire,
Prepared for quick and close affray,
Spreading abroad from common stock,
Like rays of light from central fire,
Fell o'er the naked head and face,
Cutting the skin like blades of steel.

The shot, which fired the southern heart,
Not then had gained historic fame,
But this fierce blow one southern heart,
And brain and nervous force and hand,
Stirred, as no cannon peal could move.
His hand, rolled to an iron maul,
Leaped forth like bomb from mortar's throat,
Propelled by fierce explosive force.
The driver's face was in its path.
A moment, and a prostrate form
Was quivering, bleeding, on the earth.
The prince unto his cabin walked.

A mutiny on board a ship,
A traitor spy within the camp,
Conspiracy to seize the throne,
And reigning dynasty destroy,
Discovered train and burning fuse,
Leading to powder magazine:
These none or all could wake alarm,
Amid the circles where revealed,

As that fierce blow of vengeful wrath
Aroused among those lowly ones.
  A creeping horror thence outspread,
As waves from central sinking stone.

  The morrow's sun saw both in place.
  The one with basket in his hand,
Commencing his accustomed work;
The blood-red seams on face and neck,
Showing the fiery track the lash
Had cut, when passion ruled the hand.
  Yet bearing still his head erect,
And eyes undropped before his foe.

  The other walked with sullen air,
His face was swollen, bruised, and sore,
The eyes inflamed, and nearly hid
By the o'erhanging blackened brows,
Whose darkened circles met beneath.
  The lips were cut upon the teeth,
And teeth were shattered from their place.
  His whip was held with trembling hand,
While free exposed to sight of all,
The silver decked revolvers shone.
  Their eyes met once, no word was spoke,
No threatening motion each to each,
And yet each saw, in other's eyes,
A will unbroke, determined, strong.
  The one determined ne'er to bow,
Or take the lash from other's hand.
  The other, strong in passion's force,
Malignant, treacherous, cruel, coarse,
His wounded pride to madness stung,
His blazing fury only waits
For time to glut ferocious hate;
With studied art and measured pain,
To grind beneath his feet the man
Who dared withstand his passion's course.

And through that cowed and fearful throng
The whispered terror daily spread,
And dreadful stories of the past,
Of shrieks and screams of mangled ones,
Who cut by whips or burned with fire,
Or torn by dogs with bloody fangs,
Or starved, or shot, or drowned, or flayed,
Made expiation for their crimes.

These horrid tales at dead of night,
Or whispered each to each by stealth,
Filled all the air with nameless fear;
As when of old the sheeted dead
Did gibber in the streets of Rome.
They knew the sleeping storm would break;
That power only bides its time.

The crimes of unrestricted power,
Their actors ever justified,
By prating public order's need.
For this the massive prison walls,
And fetid dungeon's cold embrace;
The ax of executioner,
Its polished surface stained with blood;
Another name for tyrant's will.
And Slavery's realm of lawless power
Examples made, vindictive, swift,
Of those who dared transgress his laws.

The council sat; a court unique;
The master and his hired thrall:
No ancient sacred forms and robes,
No ermine shining on the brow,
No book containing written code,
No oath the witness' conscience binds:
No juror, sitting in his place,
Sifting from falsehood grains of truth.

No advocate to shield the weak,
And slandered innocence defend;
But power despotic sits in court,
With Slavery's precedents to guide.
  These ever say, Crush out the will,
Refractory ones must be subdued,
Whate'er the cost, e'en unto death.
  One witness standing in that court,
A swollen, blackened, battered face,
Like index finger, pointed plain
To dangers Slavery ever feared.

  The mandates of the court were these:
The offending slave, his naked flesh
Three hundred lashes shall receive.
  The burning iron on his hand
Shall brand the memory of his deed.
  The iron yoke, with pointed prongs,
Its burden on his shoulders pressed,
Shall then be locked about his neck.
  A chain, with heavy ball attached,
Shall on his ankle then be locked,
Which he shall wear in house and field.
  Thus all from him shall lesson learn,
How sharp and sure the punishment
For hands against a white man raised.

  A Sabbath morning broke on earth;
The city's roar to quiet hushed,
The rolling wheel and creaking mill,
The toiling engine's labored breath,
Have ceased to vex the burdened air.
  The gates of labor's temple closed,
The saw and plane and hammer rest.
  The place of trade, of court, of school,
Have ceased to echo hurrying feet.
  And Sabbath oil has soothed the waves,
Which late in furious anger rolled.

The cloud fleets of the upper deep,
Waiting the breezes, lie becalmed;
And sunshine finds no trembling leaf,
To spatter broken rays of light
On mossy bank or glassy pool;
But earth and air, and cloud and tree,
Are bathed in ocean depths of peace.

Then music of the Sabbath bells,
With varied cadence charms the ear,
And organ tones, sublime and full,
Perfumed with beauty, sweetness, love,
Send out their calls to house of prayer.
And soon, from out the city's throngs,
And gathered from the village street,
From mountain side and vale and plain,
They hasten to the temple gates,
Whose spires like taper fingers point,
Through storm and calm, by day and night,
Tow'rd the unseen Eternal One.
They tread with joy these hallowed courts,
And words of prayer and songs of praise
Lift upward to th' immortal heights.
O glorious Sabbath, day of peace!
Glad bridal of the earth and heaven.

But Sabbath hours saw other scenes:
The cotton gathered from the field,
The day of rest returned again;
For some a day of festal mirth,
With drink and smoke, and feast and song,
And viler deeds were often wrought
Before the face of noonday sun.

The invitation notes sent forth;
The masters, drivers, leading ones,
Were gathering on the Sabbath morn.
The last to witness scourge and pain,

And torture by the burning brand,
Then bear, to those who home remained,
The terror that these deeds inspired.

   They come with horses, dogs, and guns,
With passions fed by maddening draught,
With grim delight, and threat and curse,
Like vulture scenting far a corse,
Till scores are gathered in the band.
   One cabin, from the early morn,
Had been close watched by vengeful eyes.

   The focus of this gathering storm
Was well aware of its approach,
Was not unmindful of its wrath;
He saw the sun mount up the sky,
The vast expanse which o'er him hung,
Glowing with peaceful heavenly light.
   The fields, with emerald carpets spread,
The brook meandering through the vale,
The trees majestic in their strength,
The mountains standing in their might.
   But 'mid it all he saw no friend,
And all he knew of God or man,
Or State, or Church, he only knew
That all combined his soul to crush.

   He stood before the cabin door,
Beleaguered by his murderous foes.
   He saw the maddened crowd draw nigh,
As wolves surround a stag at bay,
No pity in their demon eyes.

   But still his soul refused to yield;
Like philosophic atom, strong,
No power without could force its gates,
Or break its adamantine walls.
   One thought, like fire, burned in his soul,
And filled each fiber of his frame.

No white man's hand should touch his form,
Or bind his free unfettered limbs.
That lash and blow the chain had broke.
Thus born anew to manhood's state,
With freedom's wine intoxicate,
His birthright none from him should rob.

"Put down your arms and cross your wrists,"
Said one, approaching with a rope.
Those brazen knuckles flew once more,
And one man's arms were dropped in haste;
When, like an arrow from the bow,
Or cannon-shot through forest trees,
He broke through the surrounding crowds,
Scattering his foes from out his path,
As children flee from frightened horse,
Straight as an arrow for the swamp.
Horses and dogs pursue in vain,
Pistols and rifles miss their mark.
He gains the margin of the pool.
Down, down, into its silent depth,
Unwhipped, unbound, unburned, unchained,
His freedom's birthright thus maintained.

Rest, noble, brave, heroic man,
Rest quiet in thy liquid grave,
And on that morn, when earth and sea
Shall yield their dead, thine ear shall hear
The resurrection angel's voice.

Among these oft-recurring scenes,
Where broken households, blighted hopes,
Torture of body and of soul,
Like clouds of darkness filled the land;
There also mingled rays of light.
When human help and hope were gone,
The soul, in these terrific straits,

Poured forth its agonizing cry
To Him, who, making quest for blood,
Forgetting not the humble ones,
Deliverance gave from threatened doom.
    An instance of such prayer attend.

    Kentucky! famous middle land,
The ancient hunting-ground of BOONE,
Thy soil and climate, hills and vales,
Thy stalwart sons, and daughters fair,
Have given thee an honored name.
    Thy noble statesman's clarion voice
Revealed the sweet and silver tone
Which could be wrought from polished CLAY.
    And 'mid thy fertile harvest fields
The bondman's yoke most lightly pressed,
While Christian worship, prayer, and song
Gilded the iron chains they wore.

    A mighty preacher of his race
For many days his camp had held
Near the great river's rolling floods;
And sable crowds, for many miles,
Had waited on his burning words,
Till on their dark, untutored souls,
The awful thoughts of sin and death,
Of God most holy, just, and high,
Of judgment and eternal scenes,
Of mercy found in Jesus' blood,
Had wakened every slumbering sense,
Till awe and fear and hope and joy
To utmost verge, each bosom filled.
    Still as of old, 'mong sons of God,
Did Satan's presence mar their peace.

    The evening worship had commenced,
And shouts and songs were rising high,
When preacher's voice broke on the air.

"Let singin', shoutin', stop at once,
No time for singin', shoutin', now,
But time for lamentation, prayer,
Our brudder, Sam, was sold to-day,
And down dark ribber he must go,
Unless our God shall break de chains,
And free him from de trader's hand."

The noise was in a moment hushed,
And every knee was bent in awe,
While preacher's lips this prayer poured forth:
"O Lord! we are a people poor;
O Lord! thou know'st we are despised;
O Lord! how sore we are oppressed,
Yet, Lord, we are thy people still.
And now regard our bitter cry,
And grant our brudder may be free
From de bad trader's wicked hands,
From de dark ribber down to death."

And thus, with words of anguish deep
And stormy sorrow's broken breath,
Mingled with humble, trusting faith,
His cry to God went strongly forth.
When hush! a sudden silence falls;
He waits a moment, to discern
The voice that whispers in his soul;
Then, rising, with electric bound,
With flashing eye and brow uplift,
With outstretched arm and clenchéd hand,
He cries in loud impassioned tones:
"Arise! arise! and praise de Lord,
And shout and sing his blessed name,
I have a message from de skies,
A telegraphic 'spatch from God,
Borne on de wires from heaben to earf,
Writ on de table ob my heart.
It says that Sam shall be redeemed;

De trader's gold shall nebber buy;
He from down ribber shall be sabed.
　Arise! arise! and praise de Lord,
And shout and sing his glorious name."
　The lamentation strains now ceased,
And hallelujahs smote the air.

　A day had passed; a slight event—
An accidental trifle deemed
By those who see no hidden hand
Weaving the threads of mortal life—
Had broken the unfinished sale,
And from the trader Sam returned.
　Another evening had the camp
Convened for sermon, song, and prayer,
When Sam into the assembly came.
　Then preacher's voice broke forth anew:
"I told you, brudders, I receibed
A telegraphic 'spatch from God."
And then, with soul enwrapt, he cries:
　"Our God, de Lord, de mighty God,
Can sabe his own from gates of hell;
He holds de tunders in his fists
And troo his fingers, pressin' out,
Dare streams de lightnin's ob de heabens.
　O praise de Lord! he hears our cries,
And sends deliberance from de skies."

　From wise and prudent ones are hid,
While to the humble are revealed
The counsels of Immortal Powers.

　In burden of the Hebrew seer,
Called to proclaim the coming doom
Of Nineveh, so proud and great—
The bloody city, full of lies,
Assyria's ancient capital—
Amid the tempests raining forth,

Of whirlwind, earthquake, flood, and fire,
He saw the vision some have deemed
The picture of our modern time;
The chariots raging in the streets,
And jostling each in the broad ways,
While flaming torches wide illumed
Their lightning pathways through the land.

The watcher, at the midnight hour,
Waiting the coming of his foes,
Laying his ear upon the earth,
Discerns afar the tramping feet.
So, bending down our ears, we hear
The myriads of rolling wheels,
The clang of bells, the puffs, the screams,
The thundering of a thousand trains,
Which, like the blazing starry spheres,
Go sweeping o'er their iron ways.

They pass across the open plain,
They thread the river's sinuous path,
They rise along the mountain's side,
Leaping across the awful chasms,
Winding among the wooded heights,
And on, and on, 'mid harvest fields,
Past farm-house, hamlet, town and stream,
With never-ending rush and roar.

From eastern cities thronged, they pass
Across the Alleghany's heights;
Or else along the open way,
Where Indian chiefs built council fires;
Flying Niagara's awful depths,
Thence skirting coasts of inland seas,
Scaling the cloud-capped mountain heights
Which hide their precious stores below,
Plowing Sierra's drifted snows;

Then, charmed with golden harvests' breath,
They only rest by ocean shore.

The nation's life blood, through these veins
From day to day, doth ceaseless flow.
This circulation, healthful, free,
The nation's pulse beats even, strong,
Obstructed, fevered, or impaired,
Then soon is heard financial groans.

Amid these thousand thundering trains
Which give to tens of thousands bread,
And welfare-touch of millions more,
One road there was, well known by name,
And not without some meed of fame,
Which never named its officers,
Or told the starting of its trains.
But few its place of business knew,
Its office doors seemed always closed,
And agent never could be found.
Its shares no market value had,
And were not known at brokers' boards.
But still its business flourished well.
No bonds or mortgage on its lines,
Writs nor injunctions could not stay
Its trains, when signaled to depart.
It had monopoly of trade.
It was the railroad under-ground.

The trains all run from South to North;
Its southern terminus was found
In house and shop, in wood and field,
Where passengers, who took this line,
Were latest seen, then seen no more.
Its northern terminus was built
Beyond the spacious inland seas,
Illumed and cheered by sunlight smile,
Beneath the blood-red English cross,

Which floats in triumph o'er its domes,
Temple and palace all in one.
  A palace: long-sought place of rest
For weary, friendless, hunted ones.
  A temple: where the first free air
To God was breathed in praise and prayer.

  The trains, which ran the under-ground,
When using tracks of other roads,
Were run in shadow o'er these lines;
By only few their passage seen.
  A few examples may suffice.

  One bright midsummer, early morn,
An Indiana river town,
Beside Ohio's rolling floods,
Beheld a carriage pass its streets
And stop before its chief hotel.
  Two gentlemen had seats within,
The luggage fastened on the rack,
While seated by the driver's side,
A negro servant had a place.
  Th' obsequious waiter from the inn
The gentleman assisted down.
  The waiter and the servant bore
The luggage to the hall within.
  The curious gapers, gathering round,
The friendly conversation heard
Between the friends about to part.

  One said, the coming heated weeks
He should remain in northern States,
Should visit eastern towns and mills,
Arrangements make for autumn trade;
In *Saratoga* spend a time,
To the White Mountains take a run,
Perhaps Niagara see again,

And visit old-time friends once more,
Who lived adjacent to his routes.
 This respite from his business cares
His system would with vigor tone.
 He should expect in winter months
To see his friend in *New Orleans,*
At festival of " Mardi Gras."

 The other wished a pleasant time,
Sorry that business cares forbade
Him join his friend on summer stroll,
But hoped his business would allow
A winter visit at the South.
 They took each other by the hand,
And lingered o'er the last " Good-bye."
 The carriage took one friend away.

 Entering within, the other wrote
Upon the daily register,
" HENRY DE MARS, and servant-man,"
Of *New Orleans,* and now " en route
For *Cincinnati* and the East."
 His conversation soon revealed
He from *St. Louis* recent came,
Had railroad left to see a friend,
And finding now the river near
Concluded to go on by boat.

 The midday passed, the dinner ate,
The signal of a boat was heard,
A carriage took them to the wharf,
Master and man were soon on board,
And steaming onward toward the East.
 At *Cincinnati* now arrived,
Our traveler stopped at " 'The Revere."
 The register received his name,
" HENRY DE MARS, and servant-man,
New York and *Boston* now en route."

While waiting for the evening train
The meddling abolitionists,
Who watched with jealous, eager eyes
At the hotels where Southrons stopped,
Soon saw the name upon the books,
And waiting Negro servant saw.
　The officious clerk, anxious to serve
His moneyed patrons of the South,
The master warned against the schemes
Of those who sought his slave to steal,
Pointing to one whom he declared
To be a leader in their ranks.

　To him the angry master spoke
In words more plain than courteous deemed.
　Told him to mind his own affairs;
The slaves of southern gentlemen
Were better housed and taught and fed
Than the white niggers of the North.
　His servant here none could persuade
To leave his master to be free.
Then, turning to the man, he said:
"These men pretend to be your friends,
And if you wish to go with them
Permission now I freely give;
Choose now whom you henceforth will trust."
　The slave replied: "I choose to stay
With you, whom I have always known;
My home and friends are in the South,
I do not wish to be made free."

　A penny-a-liner of the press,
Seeking the city's daily news,
Well pleased, the conference heard, and soon
Prepared, with much embellishment,
The story for the morning sheet,
Turning the laugh and scorn upon
Slave-stealing abolitionists.

When hour of evening train had come,
Our travelers to the station rode,
And sleeper for Niagara took.

As morning sun illumed the earth
The restless, rattling, hurrying train
Skirted along Niagara's course,
Contending with the watery race,
And, where the river thundering fell,
The train was halted on the brink.
   A room engaged, "HENRY DE MARS,
And servant-man, from *New Orleans,*"
Was entered on the hotel books.

   Breakfast dispatched, a carriage called,
The servant rode at driver's side,
And they went forth for morning air.
   The cooling winds from river blew,
The fields and trees wore summer dress,
The yards were filled with flowery bloom,
The well-fed horses moved in pride,
The polished whirling carriage wheels
Were flashing in the shining sun.
   The iron horse's frantic scream,
Joined with Niagara's thundering bass,
Chanted titanic harmonies;
And swiftly on the carriage rolled
Toward that woven iron web
So deftly spun and lightly hung
So high above the boiling floods.
   The horses turn across the bridge,
They reach the farther rocky bank,
They pass beneath the blood-red cross
Whose shadow changes slaves to men.
   He had no slave when he returned.

   Another day, the papers said,

Mr. De Mars, from *New Orleans*,
Had lost his servant at the falls.
He was allowed to cross the bridge,
No law compelled him to return.
   The papers said, the owner thought,
The strong attachment of his slave
Prevented all desire t' escape.
   By some, accounted added proof
Of base ingratitude of slaves;
While others thought, when freedom came,
It was not strange they freedom chose.

   Returned unto the homeward side,
A thousand-dollar chattel gone,
And some rejoicing at his loss,
The falls soon lost their power to charm.

   A later morning, Martin Stone,
Commercial traveler for a firm,
Chicago wholesale hardware house,
Came home from visit of his friends
Who lived near Massachusetts Bay.

   A later paper gave account
Of slave escaped from Tennessee,
Traced to a town in Illinois.
   The sentinels at northern posts
Were notified by telegraph.
   The routes which led toward northern towns
Were closely watched by eager eyes,
Anxious to grasp the large rewards.
   He, therefore, took the under-ground.

   One windy, chilly day in March
There passed along a country road,
Which southward led from railway town
In central part of Empire State,
Through mud and slush of wasting snows
An ill-shod, ragged, weary man.

The persons who this traveler met,
He passed with shrinking, hunted look.
 They saw the stain of Negro blood,
While features bore Caucasian type.
 From those he dared he asked the way
To reach the Methodist preacher's house.
 A day will come, that reckoning day,
When no dishonor it will bring,
That hunted, famished, fleeing ones
Within these homes protection sought.
 A rap was heard; the opened door
Revealed a tall, stern-visaged man,
Wearied and chilled with morning ride,
And not in pleasant, kindly mood
To listen to a stranger's tale.

 To question, where the preacher lived,
Reply was made, "This is the place."
 With trembling voice again he asked,
"Are you the preacher living here?"
 In tones more crisp and hard he heard,
"I am the man; what do you want?"
 The feather breaks the camel's back;
These words, whose tones so harsh repelled,
Where hopes had struggled 'gainst his fears,
Were answered with a broken voice,
Where hope was yielding to despair:
 "Massa, if you refuse to help,
Then shoot me, but betray me not."
 One touch of nature makes all kin;
The cry a human soul gives out,
When sinking down to shoreless depths,
Can ne'er be feigned by hypocrite.
 That cry broke through the rugged wall
That there inclosed a tender heart.
 "Are you a fugitive?" he asked,
"Come in, and you shall find a friend."

We gather from the tale he told,
From *Carolina* he had come,
Hiding in hold of coastwise sloop,
Which brought her load of turpentine,
He found his way unto *New York*.
  A friend had helped him reach the ship,
And hidden him among its wares.
  The same had helped him leave again
By *Staten Island* boat, which asked
If such consignment was on board.

  This part of cargo, thus discharged,
The vessel slowly found its wharf.
  The landing made, the plank thrown out,
The marshal was the first on board,
Th' assistants guarding all escape.
  By name and right of Federal law
He came, a fugitive to claim.
  The vessel's deck, not one should leave,
Until absconding slave was found.
  From end to end, above, below,
In every nook and hiding place,
Through every box and cask and bale
A thorough search, and naught was found.

  Meantime a *Richmond* ferry-boat,
Among the hundreds daily brought
To mingle in the city's roar,
Had brought the fleeing fugitive;
And, while the marshal searched the ship,
A Hudson River Railway train
Was running forty miles an hour,
Bearing him onward toward the north.
  A message had prepared the way
For friend to meet him at the train,
At *Albany;* and for a night,
Beneath a Christian roof, he found
Shelter and rest, in Christian land.

Conductor, living in the town,
Whose morning train o'er Central Road
Had ne'er refused such passengers,
This traveler found on board his train.
 And when the morning sun arose,
The iron horse, now westward bound,
Dashed fierce along the river's bank,
Which carries still its Indian name
In memory of the wasted tribe
Which dwelt of yore amid its vales,
The Mohawk! whose impetuous flow
Still mirrors forth the passions fierce
Of the dead race whose name it bears.
 And 'mid the diverse, changing throngs,
Which filled these coaches as they passed,
Throbbing with joy or bowed with pain,
Was riding one, whose sunlit hopes
Had risen to meridian heights;
Who visions had of Freedom's climes,
As Israel had in Babylon,
Which were by ancient psalmist sung:
Within thy gates, our feet shall stand,
Jerusalem, the golden land.

 The blood-hound scent of Slavery's dogs,
Late foiled, were baying on the track.
 Lightning express at *Albany*,
The marshal brought in hot pursuit;
He found the sought-for bird had flown,
And also found those filled with greed,
Whose palms ne'er shrank from price of blood,
To tell the route and train he went.

 How rich and sweet the anthem flows,
While poetry of motion charms,
As keys are touched by fingers trained,
Which chord with symphonies within,
And from the music-burdened strings

The liquid harmonies burst forth,
Telling their tales of pain or bliss,
Stirring our passions with their breath.

But he who sits beside his desk,
And touches but a single key,
With dot and dash, and dash and dot,
Repeated oft, in varying forms,
And striking only iron string,
Sounds strains which stir the souls of men,
As highest art can never do,—
Strains, which arouse the human will,
And fan our passions to a flame;
Strains, whose delightful melodies,
Fill all the soul with sweetest joy.
And strains, so overlade with woe,
They bruise and crush and rend with pain,
They close the doors of earthly hope,
Blot out the sun and darken heaven.

A human ear caught such a strain
That morning passing o'er the wire.
Directions sent to *Utica*,
To stop and hold the hunted slave
Until pursuer had arrived.

The train had stopped; the hurrying throng
Pressed outward, o'er the platform steps,
While other throngs a moment stayed,
Then rushed within to take their place.
Conductor, standing on the ground,
With eye which ranged from front to rear,
Close watched the rapid changes made;
Yet listened, while a friend approached,
And whispered message in his ear.
The signal given, the ponderous wheels
Responded to the fiery breath,

Breathed through the monster's iron lungs,
And with a thousand giants' power
The train sped on its iron way.
   Another station reached; again
The hurrying throng their places change;
Once more the signal given to start,
And on the fiery dragon goes.
   Among those persons, one inquired
The way to "Methodist preacher's" house.
He told his tale, was straightway sent,
To brother pastor out of town.
   And thus it came, this preacher found
A living man beneath his roof,
Who plead: "If you refuse to help,
Then shoot me, but betray me not."

   To faith was joined substantial works,
The Negro, warmed and fed and clothed,
Was sheltered 'neath a friendly roof,
Until reconnoissance was made.
   When night her sable mantle spread,
A carriage started toward the east,
Bearing the fleeing fugitive,
The preacher as the charioteer.
   The hare had doubled on its track,
And Slavery's dogs were foiled again.
   The morning light the carriage found,
Near *Saratoga*, going north.
   Another morn the fleeing one
Inhaled the air slaves cannot breathe.
   He traveled by the under-ground.

   The preacher who his faith thus showed,
M'DONALD we with reverence name.
   In other days, the name had come
From heather mountains, o'er the seas,
And blood that ran within his veins,
Took tone from Scotia's mountain air.

But other scenes than these transpired,
Beneath the ægis of the law,
Which made the North a hunting ground.
　The humble households, 'scaped from thrall,
Who dwelt within the States called free,
Were struck with terror and alarm.
　Some fled at once to *Canada*,
As partridge covey hastes to hide,
When hunter's foot, or bark of dog,
Disturbs them in their sheltering wood.
　And some, through freedom bolder grown,
Delayed to leave their toil-won homes,
Until surprised—as frightened sheep,
When wolves leap o'er the sheltering yard—
By those who, armed with law and force,
Came to devour their new-born hopes,
And bind anew their broken chains.

　Fair Susquehanna! shining stream,
From mountain springs, 'mid wooded heights,
From silver lakes, through brooks and rills,
Fed by the summer's falling showers,
And winter's stormy drifting snows;
Thy waters aye, in beauty flow:
Now rippling o'er thy graveled bed,
Now shimmering in the glassy pool,
Now dallying with thy grassy banks,
Now hastening onward in thy course,
With graceful bend and pleasant smile,
Greeting the mountains by thy path,
As beauteous maid, with tripping feet,
With silvery speech and rippling laugh,
Salutes her friends on every side.

　A perished race bequeathed thy name,
And left, on all the shining streams
That pour their waters through thy vale,
Memorials of their ancient sway.

Otsego, sleeping 'neath its shades;
Schenevus, through whose mountain paths
The iron horse first found its way,
To drink thy waters at their font;
Otego, crisp and short the sound,
And Unadilla, rolling name,
Like Indian boat rocked by its waves;
Chenango, open, smooth, and fair,
As the rich vale through which it flows.
  Canasawacta, who can tell
The import of these tones, that cut
So clear and sharp upon the ear?
And Genegantsletz, mingled tones,
Tinkling and lisping on our tongues.
  Tioughniougha, hard to speak,
As twisted roots of ancient Greek;
Tiog, Owego, and Chemung,
With many others still unsung,
Whose liquid silver, freely given,
Thy treasures and thy beauty swell.

  The valleys where these rivers flow,
With all their upland sunny slopes,
Are homes of earnest thoughtful men;
And but for blight of sin and death,
A paradise were here restored.

  Around thy earliest shining fount,
The glimmer glass of hemlock shades,
And o'er thy tangled, pathless wilds,
Mingled with memories fading now,
Of Indian braves and dusky maids,
A COOPER's witching pen has flung
Romantic fancy's shining veil.
  And where thy floods in grandeur sweep,
Along *Wyoming's* storied plains,
CAMPBELL's pellucid, radiant song
Has voiced the beauty of thy shores.

Thus, from thy early solitudes,
From wandering shades, of perished race,
From echoing axes, first to ope
The paths of sunshine on thy banks,
And later, from thy cultured fields,
From dwellers in thy vales and towns,
And travelers through thy open gates,
By painter's brush, and pen and song,
The voices all combine to say:
Fair Susquehanna! shining stream,
Flow on in splendor to the sea.

One tragedy our song reveals,
In which these waters, fresh and sweet,
Were plashed with blood, by Slavery shed.
 Adjacent to that granite shaft,
Which marks the place of ancient strife,
Where settlers fell by murderous foe,—
" Wyoming massacre," 'tis named,—
Upon the river's eastern bank,
WILKESBARRE stands. A fugitive,
In days gone by, here found a home;
While Freedom's brimming cup of joy
Sweetened the bread his hands had earned.

 The hounds of Slavery tracked him out,
The bludgeon first their presence told.
 Staggering beneath the cruel blow,
Which failed of its designed effect,
To lay their victim at their feet,
One cry of pain, one startled glance
Into the faces of his foes,
He bounds away; as when a buck
Is wounded by the hunter's shot,
No covert on the land, he rushed
Straight to the river's sheltering arms.
 Behind was death, or bondage sore,
While Freedom challenged death before.

His foes stopped at the water's edge,
They would not risk for meed of gold
What he had risked for liberty.
  But while he struggled with the wave,
They poured on him their murderous fire.
  And when their deed of death was done,
And helpless body floating down,
They then with scorn and cursing cried,
They for dead niggers had no use.

  Apostate ones, among the damned,
Who lure the souls of men astray,
Gather the harvests of their work;
But human devils leave their prey,
When utmost ruin they have wrought.

  Through all this fiercely raging strife
One noble State in grandeur stood,
Unswerving, in her constant love
Of liberty and human right;
Not all alone, but foremost still.
  With port majestic, eye serene,
And clarion voice resounding far,
Though statesmen, poets, and divines,
And orators of matchless tone,
Her feet unmoved from freedom's base
On *Plymouth rock* and Faneuil Hall,
As WEBSTER points, with outstretched hands,
" 'Tis *Massachusetts;*" there she stands.

  But in the bitter days we tell,
When Slavery wielded Federal law,
Her beauteous robes were trailed in dust,
Her golden crown was dashed to earth;
While on her freedom-loving streets,
Past Faneuil Hall, now draped in crape,
Past General Court, now stricken dumb,
Past halls of justice, bayonet barred,

The ranks of Federal troops moved on
Guarding one chained and helpless man.
 The wharf was reached, the plank thrown out,
The deck was gained, beneath the flag
Known round the world as Freedom's hope;
Yet waving here o'er black-mouthed guns,
And men in arms, to crush the free.
 And o'er the waters pilgrims sailed
To find a home from tyrants free,
And o'er the waves historic made,
Where freemen spurned a tax on tea,
They bore away the captured one,
And SIMS became historic name.

 South Carolina! fiery State,
Which threatened oft to nullify
Acts and decrees of Federal power.
 Who from the tilts in senate halls—
Her champions eager for the fray
With *Massachusetts*' honored son—
Angry and bleeding bore their wounds.
 Who drove with violence from her soil
An honored citizen, who came
To test her Slavery-fashioned laws
Before the nation's highest court.
 The State which trained the assassin's hand,
Which smote a SUMNER in his place,
And used the bludgeon argument
To answer words for Freedom spoke;
She sought to soothe her wounded pride,
And mortify a rival State,
And used the arm of union law
To tear a freeman from his home,
And bear him to his chains again.

 Thus have we told, as words can tell,
The overflowing cup of woe,
Pressed to the lips of those enslaved.

But words are feeble, soulless things,
To measure out the agonies
Wrung, drop by drop, from suffering ones,
To utmost bound of human life.
The fire consuming living flesh,
The iron grinding through the bones,
The nameless horrors souls endure
When pierced by Slavery's poisoned fangs,
None e'er can know but those who feel.

Have told the same, as blades of grass
Doth tell the vastness of the plain,
As single drops tell falling rains
Which spread o'er half a continent,
Or dippings of an infant's hand
Can measure out Atlantic deeps.
So dark and dreadful is this woe,
So vast and high this crime doth reach,
No tongue or pen can tell its pain.
But evermore, like ocean waves,
Its calmest moods hath restless tones,
While oft its seething foaming deeps,
Which rise and toss themselves on high,
Their victims dash on rocks of death,
And overflow the solid ground
Of justice, truth, and righteousness.

'Tis well a voice divine has spoke:
"Thus far, no farther, shalt thou go,
And here let thy proud waves be stayed."

IX.

THE AWAKENING.

MYSTERIOUS sleep; eclipse of life;
Return of ante-natal dawn,
Wherein the soul unconscious rests,
Waiting the summons to arouse.
Emblem of darkness, erst was said
By voice divine, "Let there be light."
Yet prophecy of strength renewed,
When joint and axle fully oiled,
And every fiber full in tone,
Shall answer back in quick response
The mandates of the active will.

The self-existing needs thee not;
Created ones, e'en morning stars,
Have times of rising and of rest.

While sailing o'er these unknown seas,
Where sounding-line was never cast,
No chart or star to guide the bark,
No light within the binnacle,
To note the warder pointing north;
No sound of bell o'er sunken rock,
Or clarion horn amid the night,
To tell the dangers drawing nigh;
But all is dark, unformed, unknown.
One eye alone this realm explores,
To whom the darkness is as light.
He guides through all these trackless wastes
To solid ground of conscious life.

Unto those unseen powers which bind,
Harmonious, all terrestrial things,—
Termed Gravitation, Light and Heat,
Magnetic and Electric force,—
Which trend so near organic life,
We add another—waking force,
Egiroism—subtle power,
Born of conjunction of the stars,
Or sifted from ethereal heights,
When reached by rays of morning sun,—
Which, entering portals of the flesh,
Touching the mystic cords that bind
The body and the spirit one,
Begets anew a living soul.
    This force, like others we have named,
Another channel, through which flows
The quick'ning of Eternal power.

    Not less profound and dark, the sleep
Of moral sense. The conscience drugged
By love of power, by avarice,
And many forms of sin, which spring
Spontaneous in the human soul.
    And only breath divine, which first
Awoke unconscious clay to life
Amid these stupors, dense and foul,
Can rouse and purify the sense
Which doth distinguish good and ill.

    And while the nation slept o'er crime,
While greed and passion, power and law,
Welded the chains the bondman wore,
The breath of God again went forth,
Till conscience, quickened by the touch,
And crying in its pain, awoke.

    'Twas thus in other days: a youth,
Ingenuous, earnest to excel,

With literary pride inspired,
Sought *Alma Mater's* laurel wreath ;
His thesis was the slave-trade shame.
　　He studied, pondered, reasoned, wrote,
Enlarged, explained, revised again,
Still striking out each useless word,
And strongly welding thought to thought,
Until the wealth of every lore,
The grandeur of the argument,
The classic diction, beauty, force,
Combined to win the sought-for prize.
　　But while his genius, learning, wit,
And all his powers were thus employed,
A force divine within had wrought
A slumbering conscience to awake.
　　He found, now standing at his gates,
A knight whose armor flashed in light,
Demanding throne and crown within.

　　But selfish interests claimed his life;
And love of ease, of pleasure, fame,
Hung out their shining crowns to view,
While conscience, clanging at the bars,
Was ringing through his soul these words:
"The battle with these powers of hell
Some one must fight, and why not thou?"
　　The conflict of the storm-tossed soul,
Ended with conscience on the throne.
　　And CLARKSON cast away his gloves,
And bared his youthful arms for fight,
Joining his blows with WILBERFORCE,
And other champions for the right,
Nor stayed his hands, till England's flag
O'er slave-ship never more could wave.

　　Who are the heroes of the earth?
Where are the valiant, worthy men,

Whose names have right to be inscribed
Upon the role of deathless ones ?
   Immortal stars! whose steady light
Shall shine undimmed from age to age.
   Are they the men whose hands are stained
In blood ? who, in the storms which sweep
The nations in their angry might,
Are borne upon the highest crests,
While thousands sink beneath the waves ?
Their names illumed by lurid light
Of burning cities, fields, and homes,
Mingled with screams of maddened wife,
And starving children's sighs and groans.
   Has earth no better, nobler one,
On whom to place the hero's crown ?

   Or shall the gift to gather gold,
To turn the streams from every source,
To swell the coffers, bursting now,
Until the treasure, heaped so vast,
A mountain weight doth press the heart,
And every sweet and healthful juice
Is slow exuded drop by drop—
Leaving what else had been a home
Of kindly sympathy, of sweet
And tender sensibility,
Of love for friend and child and wife,
Only a piece of worthless waste
Which, analyzed, alone reveals
Its greed of gold and ice and dirt,—
Be counted worthy of our praise ?
   Such men should never wear a crown,
Their use is but to be forgot.

   Or shall the highly gifted ones,
The chiefs in letters, art, and song,
Whose banners float so far aloft,
That all the world their glory see,

Whose toils and treasures, free bestowed,
Oft smooth the rugged ways of life,
Or gratify the finer sense
Of beauty, wit, and harmony;
Those who from their abundance give
Of that which doth increase their store,
Who in their labor find delight
Richer than most that earth affords;
Where self receives so large a share,
Ought they to wear the brightest crowns?

We turn our eyes to humbler scenes:
To fathers toiling in their love,
Through weakness, pain, and poverty,
Providing bread for needy ones,
Without the world's inspiring praise,—
True heroes, though uncrowned on earth.

Or when the house-band's strength, which held
The tender plants, in early youth,
Close to the central queen of home,
Is by Death's sickle cut in twain,
Leaving the unbound sheaf to waste;
What glory then should gild her brow
Who, of her trust by death despoiled,
Hushing the moans of breaking heart,
Clasps close, within her sheltering arms,
Her helpless babes. Though flesh is weak,
The willing mind shrinks not from pain
To guard and guide, to help and keep,
Those who, save her, had not a friend.

The rich were in their purple clothed,
Surrounded by their works of art,
By elegance and luxury,
Perfumes and music, pictures, books,
And journeying oft from place to place,

With friends and treasures ever new ;
Their lives seemed like a paradise.

But she, to whom the burden came
Of laboring for the orphaned ones,
Had eye and ear and heart and taste,
And could have found as sweet delight
In drinking from luxurious founts
As those who quaffed them day by day.
But daily toil consumed her strength,
And cold and hunger oft she knew,
Walking the stormy path with Him
Who, torn and bleeding, sick and faint,
Could not save self, and others save.
Only one spring of human joy,
From fountain of maternal love,
Flowed o'er her dreary waste of life.

The eyes of selfish ones but saw
A toiling woman, weak and worn,
The brightness faded from her life;
But purer vision clearly saw
An angel veiled, a heroine,
For whom there waits a fadeless crown.

Another type of hero mark:
A name unknown to human fame;
His travail no deliverance wrought;
His battles always seemed defeats;
No golden crown or laurel wreath
Adorned or shamed his modest brow.
Not moved by love of wife or child,
But like the wondrous Nazarene,
The lonely, suffering ones he sought,
And from their crushed and bleeding forms
He strove to lift the mountain weight;
But strove in vain. Thus struggling died,
And was forgot. And still unknown,

Save only by inquiring ones
Who, standing on the river's brink,
Their footsteps turn to find its source.
   And passing o'er the fertile plains,
And through the narrow sinuous vales,
And climbing slow the mountain glens,
Through tangled wood, o'er bog and rock,
They find at last the parent spring,
Where first its waters kiss the light.

   'Mong demigods of modern time,
Whose mighty martial deeds have throned
Their names among the stars of light,
Stands WINFIELD SCOTT, of *Lundy's Lane.*
   Thus welded in the battle fire,
These names for evermore are joined.

   But in the conflicts which we tell,
Lundy is more than name of place.
   It stands for hero, saint, divine.
   For one who poor, despised, unknown,
With God-like vision saw the crime
Which crushed the souls by Christ redeemed.
   From east to west, from south to north,
He traveled, prayed, and spoke and wrote,
To rouse the nation from its sleep;
And waken justice, truth, and love,
To stanch the wounds of bleeding men.

   BENJAMIN LUNDY was the name,
Within whose soul a fountain rose,
Which, swelling in its onward flow,
Became a river vast and deep,
To cleanse a continent from sin.

   Reverent we speak another name.
   A youth, with generous gifts endowed,

His lips touched with anointing fire,
Went forth to do his Master's work.
　Amid the gathering tides of men,
At confluence of the streams which swell
The mighty Mississippi's floods,
He found a home; and, true to God,—
Freedom of speech by law assured,—
He spoke in thoughtful, earnest words
Of blight and danger, Slavery brought
To the great State wherein he dwelt.
　They drove him hence. Shaking the dust
By Slavery stained from off his feet,
He sought a home on Freedom's soil,
And found a slavery-poisoned air
Which weakened every moral force,
And all the powers of ill inflamed.

　And when they sought to stop his pen,
And hush his truthful, burning words,
Or drive him from their coasts—and failed,
The shot was fired! His voice was still!
And ALTON, for this fiendish act,
Immortal infamy attained!
While LOVEJOY's name was placed on high,
Among the glorious northern stars
Which ne'er shall fade, and never set.

　And GARRISON, whose youthful days
Were spent among the toiling ones,
He early saw the flagrant crime
Of making merchandise of men,
And saw, with bitterness and pain,
Provisions in organic law
Which recognized the dreadful shame.
　The Constitution, first ordained
Union and freedom to secure,
Palladium of our liberties,

In sinewy Saxon words, he styled
"Compact with death and league with hell."
  Thus earnest, fearless, radical,
He following had, and helped to swell
The rivers sweeping o'er the land.

  And WENDELL PHILLIPS, orator
Of matchless fame, his burning words
Like molten metal swiftly flowed.
  His furnace fires were richly fed
With justice, love, and scorn, and hate,
With logic, fancy, humor, wit,
Enriched with learning's widest store;
Kindled with heated blast of truth,
The burning torrent onward poured.
  Thus rivaling the world-wide known
Philippics of Demosthenes!
  Yet running, with such oil of art,
Such liquid melody of speech,
That those, who sought to veil their shame
With softly-spoken pleasant name,
While listening to his scorching tones,
Burning the marrow in their bones,
Declared those lips with sweetness wet,
Machine infernal to music set.
  His words increased the fiery stream
Of indignation, rising fast,
Pouring against the hoary walls
Which shielded long this dreadful crime.

  And gentle-hearted WHITTIER,
Whose soul was filled with love and peace,
His flowing numbers swelled the stream.
  His eye was quick to recognize
The beauty of the plainer things.
  His ear, amid the wild refrain,
Caught minor chords of woe and pain.

The sighs and groans of breaking hearts
He gathered up, and gave them voice.
And sternest truths of righteousness,
Thundering against the oppressor's power,
He wreathed with beauty and with grace.

As keys that open long-closed doors
Are oiled to pass the rusted guards,
And swords that cut with keenest edge
Are sharped and polished for the work,
So WHITTIER's song so smoothly flowed,
It found its way through hardened hearts,
And while the ears of men were charmed,
The heart was touched and conscience roused.
The sword of truth, whose hilt he held,
Through joint and marrow found its way.

Among the prophets, thundering loud,
His was Isaiah's seraph voice;
And when the Gospel's fullness came,
His was the voice of loving John.
While trumpets, voices, broken seals,
Earthquakes and tempests, noise and flame,
Showed old things passing swift away,
He gladly hailed the earth made new,
And saw the rainbow round the throne.

And GERRIT SMITH, philanthropist,
A man of peace; of generous gifts
To needy ones; and, Dorcas-like,
Full of good works and loving deeds,
With heart as guileless as a child,
He saw the bondman in his chains,
And saw a brother needing help.
He heard the loud, distressful cry,
And all his soul with pity moved,
Commanding voice and pen and purse.

With largest welcome he received
The fleeing ones beneath his roof;
And kindled thus a beacon light,
Whose rays streamed over cotton fields,
And shone within the darkened huts.

Some thought him dreamer, others saw
A Daniel, reading from the wall
The judgment records blazing there.

Another person widely known,
A journalist of highest rank,
Whose early life of wasting toil
Gave sympathy with laboring men,
And struggles of maturer life
Taught him occasion quick to seize,
And also taught the happy art
Of giving voice to others' thoughts;
He took a teacher's trusted place.
As exhalations from the earth
Return in summer's falling showers,
So thoughts and feelings, gathered wide,
Went back to cheer and stimulate,
To quicken into active power
The love of liberty and right,
Which dormant waited through the land,—
And HORACE GREELEY, and *Tribune,*
Gave to awakening millions voice,
And lessons taught to millions more.

The legends of the northern wilds,
'Mid Scotia's misty mountain tops,
Where Fingal's dark and gloomy cave
Sheltered the weird and wandering sprites,
And murky, lowering, shifting mists
Half hid the forms, in part revealed;
The listener struck with trembling awe.

And Jove, throned on Olympian heights,
Whose brow was wreathed with clouds and
    storms,
From whence his thunder-bolts leaped forth
From depths and darkness unexplored,
Sent trembling fear to gods and men.

So SUMNER stood, apart, alone,
A gloomy grandeur round him hung;
Ne'er moved by love, nor awed by hate,
But cold, serene, and stern as fate.
He forged his thunder-bolts with care,
He polished them with highest skill,
He poised them with unerring aim,
And, Jove-like, sent them on their way.
They crushed through every wall of wrong,
They plowed the solid grounds of crime,
They set in foam the seas of sin,
And Slavery's cohorts shook with fear,
With madness, malice, shame, and pain.

The blind old bard of Albion's isle,
Whose song o'erswept the hills of time,
The dark unfathomed seas of fate,
And oceans of eternity;
He saw incarnate evil squat,
Toad-like, at our first mother's ear
Seeking to find, through human sense,
An entrance-way for sin and woe.

Thus Slavery sought incarnate form
In reptile bearing human shape,—
Forever be his name unknown!—
Whose stealthy, vengeful, fatal blow
Should reach in mortal part his foe,
And stop the shower of blistering fire
Which fell broadcast through all his camps.

The murderous effort failed its mark,
But opened depths of crime to view,
Which some till then had not believed.
  The thunder, for a season, ceased;
Then crash on crash, and peal on peal,
While lightning flames illumed the sky,
Nor rested not, until the storm
Had swept the curse from earth away.

  Central New York! historic ground,
First won from pristine wilderness
By sons of those heroic sires
Who braved New England's solitudes.
  Her children were baptized in blood
At *Cherry Valley's* grassy glades,
Schoharie, and *Oriskany.*
  They gathered, from their forest homes,
To check the lion in his path,
On *Saratoga's* storied plains.
  Freedom assured, their rugged arms
Transformed the wilderness to bloom,
And desert place with roses crowned.

  The children of these early sires
Inhaled their freedom with their breath.
  The winds that o'er their mountains swept,
And forest anthems sung, were free;
The molten silver of her streams
Went singing freely toward the sea;
And every trembling forest leaf,
With waving daisies of the field,
And flowers wet with morning dew,
Said rain, and light are free to all.
  The sparrow's chirp, the eagle's scream,
The fox's bark, and bleat of deer,
The voice of storm-cloud in the sky,
Joining Niagara's thundering bass,
All chanted songs of liberty.

The heralds of the Christian faith,
Who bore a WESLEY's honored name,
Spread o'er the land like falling rains.
  By WESLEY slavery was declared
The vilest thing beneath the sun,
And when the fires of liberty,
Which smoldered long, were bursting forth,
The sons of WESLEY caught the flame.

  Amid this band one foremost stood,
With censer swinging far and high,
Scattering the burning coals of truth,
Which scorched and shriveled where they struck
The garments wrought this shame to hide,—
Thus opening to the light of day
The vileness of the form beneath.
  With scourge of braided cords he sought
To drive the traffickers in blood
Forth from the temple's hallowed gates,
And make the pavements clean once more
To greet the feet of sons of God.
  The voice divine, from human lips,
He sounded forth. He led the band,
Who pitchers broke and trumpets blew,
Sounding alarm through all the host.
  And WILLIAM HOSMER's name shall stand,
Symbol of courage, faith, and might,
Of love of freedom, truth, and right,
And harbinger of morning light.

  The stars were fighting Sisera,
While moving onward in their course;
With Deborah and with Barak joined,
The ancient Kishon swept away
His chariots and his mighty hosts.
  With all this force of heaven and earth

Was joined a blow from woman's hand—
She drove the nail that reached his life.

Thus, 'mid the gathering floods and storms,
And blazing lights which filled the sky,
A woman's heart and woman's pen
Struck the devouring beast a blow
Which helmet, shield, and temple crushed,
And stung, and burned him as with fire.

While fancy's airy wing had flown
Among the high and titled ones,
Through cities, palaces, and courts,
And oft invoking sympathy
For lords and ladies in distress
At fancied slight or jealous scorn,
She walked among the lowly born.
   In kitchen, cabin, street, and field,
She gazed into their sorrowing eyes,
She clasped their scarred and bleeding hands,
And felt the heart-throbs of their woe.
   She walked beside a fleeing form,
A mother, bearing in her arms
Her sleeping boy. For weary miles,
With pallid face and bleeding feet,
She hastened on. She saw her rush
To Death's embrace her child to save.
   She stood within the cabin doors,
And heard the words a husband spoke,
Parting from all that man holds dear
At the command which Slavery gave.
   She heard the kiss of child and wife,
And saw him leave them evermore.
   In coffle-gang, in cotton field,
Beneath the whip, the burning brand,
Beside her sister bowed in shame,
She walked, until her soul was filled
And overflowed with burning pain.

She then unto the nation spoke:
To fathers, mothers, sisters, sons,
To wife and husband, Christian men—
To all who had a human heart;
And stirred our souls as if our own
Were walking through these awful flames.
And history evermore shall know,
As Freedom's friend and Slavery's foe,
The name of HARRIET BEECHER STOWE.

A child of servile mother born
Gave proof in color of his skin,
In form and contour of his frame,
If slave-born child e'er father had,
Caucasian blood was in his veins.

A Hebrew youth once had the choice
To stand a prince of royal line,
Yet chose a suffering servile life
With kinsmen of his blood and race.
But Slavery leaves no power of choice,
And grants no claim of race or blood,
But with her hell-begotten laws
Invades the secret holy place
Where God doth mold the formless clay,
And breathes therein immortal breath,
To brand the unborn child a slave.

FREDERICK DOUGLASS, born a slave,
Yet prince by virtue of his gifts,
He fled from bondage; justified
By higher law than man had made.
He pressed into the foremost rank
Of those traduced, abused, despised
As meddling abolitionists.
With large and cultured mental field,
With rarest gifts of public speech,
A spirit sensitive and proud,

And jealous of his manhood's rights,
With Freedom's seal within him wrought,
And Freedom fleeing feet had sought,
And Freedom British gold had bought,
He walked a freeman through the land,
And struck such blows as foemen strike
When meeting robbers of their hearth,
And ravishers of wife and child.
 Not strange that bitterness and pain
Should give an accent to his tones.
 Not strange that burning words should smite
What Slavery made defense and shield.
 Not passing strange that State and Church
Should feel the temper of his steel.
 And seeing cloud-capped battlement,
Guarding approach on every side,
Not strange that in despair he cried:
"There is no help in all the land,
Save in the bondman's strong right hand."

 While kings and prophets walked in gloom,
And giants stumbled in the path,
Unto the little ones there came
The dawnings of the morning light.
 They saw that help must come from Him
Whom tides and storms and stars obey.
 With breaking hearts they cried: O, Lord!
Thy judgments holy are and true,
And righteous evermore thy ways;
But, Lord, how long before thou judge,
And blood of murdered ones avenge,
How long before the opening seals
Shall show this Babylon destroyed,
And resurrection power descend
On spirits still in prison bound?
 The answer came, a season yet
Until the times shall be fulfilled.
 Thus praying, trusting, waiting still,

They sought the breaking morning light.
Of souls like these we give a type.

SOJOURNER TRUTH, self-chosen name,
When recreating power came,
Transforming from an earthly clod
To chosen messenger of God,
In slavery born, in slavery wed,
Her children grew among the dead,
And in her black Nigritian face
No strain of lighter blood we trace;
But PROVIDENCE, which oft assigns
The metes and bounds of earthly life,
Before her placed on open door,
And, choosing rather to be free,
Her prison-house she left behind.

She entered soon another door,
An entrance-way to worlds of light,
A golden stair-way to the skies.
"I am the door," saith One divine,
Where willing souls walk in and out,
And eat and drink, in earth and heaven.
Henceforth a life of praise and prayer,
Of holy joy in inner court;
Of loving labor on the earth
In service of his suffering ones.
Henceforth within the heavenly gate,
The name of Truth, her Master's name,
Engraved on precious stone, she wore;
And, wandering 'mong the sons of men,
SOJOURNER TRUTH her name was found.
As priest she trod the holy place,
Forever veiled from eyes of flesh;
As prophet, words divine she spoke,
And visions saw of things to come.
With holy boldness she drew nigh
The King upon the judgment-seat,

And stretched her hand afar to reach
The golden scepter that she sought.

Her children were in bondage held;
She sought above the needed help;
Her prayer was phrased in wondrous words,
A mingled argument and faith:
"O, LORD, if I were rich as you,
And you were poor, as poor as I,
I'd help you, and you know I would."
She gained the help thus boldly sought,
Her children 'scaped the prison bars.

One further picture we present:
The antislavery men of old
Ne'er minced their words, nor gave pretense
Of dignity by sounding name.
Congress, assembly, parliament,
They never held. To speed their cause
Conventions rained o'er all the land.
To these oft gathered from afar
Their authors, orators, divines,
The men of might; great, earnest souls,
Whose sifted thoughts and burning words
The mass enchained. With these there came
The feebler folk, who made amends
For lack of brains by length of hair;
And doubters of the Christian faith,
With scoffers at all sacred things;
And many a mood and tense of thought
Were crystallized about this theme.

All moral truths, philosophies,
All civil codes and claims of law,
The individual rights of man,
The sources of authority,
Limits of governmental power,

Protection for the poor and weak,
And themes and theories here unnamed,
Were melted in this crucible
To find their grains of golden sand.
 Appeals to passion, pride, and fear,
To justice, right, to sympathy,
For outraged, crushed, and suffering men,
Were mingled in these high debates.
 They stirred the people like a storm,
And impress left where'er they came.

 Convention met in Faneuil Hall,
And *Boston elite* came to see.
 The magnates of the cause were there,
SOJOURNER seated on the stage,
Surrounded by the honored ones;
And DOUGLASS was the orator.
 The crowded hall, to passion wrought,
Were drinking in his thrilling words,
And answering back with cheer on cheer
His polished shafts of biting wit.
 But soon there came a graver strain—
A picture dark as night was drawn:
The millions toiling in their bonds,
While law and custom, Church and priest,
And love of ease and greed of gold,
And pride and prejudice and power
Combined to keep them in their chains.
 And as the picture darker grew
The audience, spell-bound, held their breath,
While vision of the orator,
Sweeping across these troubled seas,
Could see no light, or hope, or help
Save in the black man's strong right hand.
 A voice in weird and startling tone
The speaker held, and thrilled each ear:
" FREDERICK ! is God—dead ?
I had not heard that God was dead."

God was not dead. SOJOURNER saw
This glorious truth. She heard his voice
Resounding through the ages past,
Proclaiming liberty to all,
And with the vision of a seer
She saw the opening prison doors.

But time and space will fail to tell
Ten thousand faithful shining ones,
Whose precious memories, ever green,
Would well befit historic page,
Or find a place in poet's song.
   Their record is the accomplished work.
   Their toil and prayer were interwrought,
Till millions flamed with quenchless fires.

X.

SKIRMISHES OF THE GREAT CONFLICT.

THE rolling tides of living men
   First filled the broad Atlantic slope,
   Then, scaling Alleghany's heights,
Had poured in never-ceasing floods
Throughout the Mississippi vale,
Thence onward o'er its mighty plains,
Still rolling toward the setting sun;
The northern waters clear and bright,
The South had Slavery's inky stain.

   The mighty conflicts of the earth,
Where empires meet in battle shock,
And throne 'gainst throne is fiercely hurled,
Wherein the issue of the strife
O'er half the world controls the life
Of nations and of centuries,
Within a small area are fought.
   Babylon, Persia, Greece, and Rome,
Each in its turn was overthrown,
As battles wage, to victory turned.
   Between the rise and set of sun
Napoleon's empire toppled down
On bloody field of Waterloo.
   The Malakoff of Russian power
O'erspread but little breadth of land;
This falling, empires' bounds were changed.
   A battle lost was Eden lost,
And earth was filled with sin and death.

And over Judah's mountains wild,
In person of the sinless One,
Redemption for the world was gained.
   Thus world-wide forces often meet,
And battle join in narrow space.

   Through compact, called a compromise,
The broad and fertile *Kansas* plains
Had been to Freedom full assured.
   Then Slavery's ever-greedy maw
The wage of compromise secured,
Demanded the remaining share;
And over this the issue joined.

   Discussion raged both fierce and long
In Congress halls. And through the land,
Awakened now, the hot words rung
From platform, pulpit, pen, and press
Against the stealthy efforts made
To sanction, with the forms of law,
This robbery of Freedom's dower.
   But words are worth but what they weigh,
And earthly compacts, treaties, laws,
Are all made up of human words.
   These words with some have moral weight;
And ought outweighs the sun and stars,
While others gauge the weight of words
By weight of powder and of ball.
   The conflict of so many years
Was passing from the stage of words;
And men were searching now to see
What was behind the words they used.

   But Slavery always stood on force,
A synonym for power and crime.
   And when she failed to rob by stealth
Her trumpet called for men in arms
To take possession of the land,

And with the bludgeon, fire, and sword
To drive the sons of Freedom out.

 But Freedom's bugles wide were blown,
And from the freedom-loving North
They hastened to their brothers' side;
Men who, like Cromwell's soldiers, stern,
Could pray and keep their powder dry.
 And in this conflict freemen learned
That force of wrong must be o'ermatched
By force that dares to stand for right.
 The wild foray was hot and fierce,
Her towns were by the flames devoured,
And many slept the sleep of death.
 But *Kansas* kept her freedom crown,
The freemen were not driven out.
 Her story may be briefly told:
Convulsions seized her embryo frame,
And periled life ere birth-hour came.
 Born 'mid the kindlings of that fire,
Designed to be a nation's pyre,
Contending factions o'er her fought,
To win her hand they fiercely sought.
 By drought and famine, scourged with pain,
By locust swarms devoured again,
While passing thus beneath the rod,
She clung to freedom and to God;
Till now rich harvests crown her plains,
And smiling plenty o'er her reigns,
The earlier trials passed from sight,
Her star is rising, clear and bright.

 Tiberius Cæsar reigned at Rome,
And Herod ruled in Galilee,
When through the wilderness there came
A "voice" which cried: "The way prepare,
Make straight the path for King of kings,
Who free to all salvation brings."

While Slavery proudly sat her throne,
Vicegerents ruling through the land,
Another "John" baptizing came,
John C. Fremont the herald's name;
And millions through this clarion voice
Were called to make the better choice,
And with his name borne wide and high,
The Freedom blasts cleared northern sky,
And when the Fates had struck the hour,
The great deliverer came in power.

And when the land bewildered stood,
Amid convulsive agonies,
Again, in desert wastes, was heard
A " voice" which cried, "The way prepare,
Lo! Freedom cometh! all rejoice!
Be wise and make the righteous choice."

Fremont! prophetic morning star,
The *avant-courier* of the sun,
The herald of the mighty voice
Which thundered forth, "The work is done!"

When from their ancient caves the winds
Break forth upon the ocean deeps,
Then restless, howling, hungry waves
Rush madly forth to hunt their prey.

They close around the struggling bark,
And, breaking it with mighty blows,
'Tis swallowed in remorseless depths.

And sometimes gallant ship is caught
And dashed against the rocky wall,
Its broken fragments strew the sea,
Or lifted high on sandy beach,
To bleach and molder in the sun.

So waves of human passions rise,
And roll and toss themselves aloft,
And bear upon their highest crests
Impulsive, earnest, hopeful men,

Sometimes to place and power and fame,
Sometimes to death, with pain and shame.

The skilled commander feels his way
O'er moat, morass, and abatis,
And o'er the wall, with hope forlorn.
And those who lead in desperate straits
Are leaders oft foredoomed to death.
The great crises of human life
Demand a human sacrifice,
A free-will offering must be found.

An even thread of life is spun,
Time draws it forth through days and years,
And toil and care, and fear and pain,
With prayer and praise are intertwined.
Domestic joys and hopes and loves
Are textiles wrought into this strand.
It seems to have no wondrous strength.
But He alone, who knew the weight
Of truth and love and righteousness
Inwrought into that quiet life,
Could see its strength. It never failed.

But when the stranded ship at night
Was struggling in the jaws of death,
The seas were running mountains high,
And rocks and shrouds were mailed with ice,
While every broken water-drop
Rained bullets on the frozen shore,
And lights were out, and cries and screams
Were mingled with the roaring blast,
He was the man to grasp the rope,
Or dare to board the sinking ship.
Or when the greedy sheet of flame
Had wrapped the house from base to dome,
And tongues of fire were shooting out
From doors and windows every side,

And stifling smoke and scalding steam
Were waiting to destroy his life,
'Twas his to climb the blistered walls,
To dare the blazing, crumbling floors,
To snatch from death a helpless one.
From dangers of exploded mine,
Where sulphurous deaths are walking free,
From frightened horse, from railway train
Which crashes through a broken bridge,
Wherever human help can reach,
His arm is ready for the work.

Such was the subject of our sketch,
JOHN BROWN, who bore no classic name,
JOHN BROWN, unknown to human fame.
Through years of youth and early prime,
The stream of life flowed quietly;
While daily care met daily want,
And sons were born, to manhood grew,
And business cares came on apace,
While east and west he journeyed forth,
And grew familiar with the land.

The eyes that turn from heavenly light,
Purblind and blinking by the lamps
Called science, nature, order, law,
Are searching through the ooze and mist
To find the genesis of man.
The son of Amram, Hebrew seer,
Whose sharpened vision looked beyond
The reach of sense, uprising saw,
And walking forth in majesty
And grandeur, like the morning stars,
A MAN! in whom was breath of lives.
A life of nature, life of sense,
Of thought, affection, memory, will,
Immortal, spiritual, divine,
Conjoined and built on base of clay.

Not wondrous strange, when dowered thus,
That man should live a dual life.
And thus with him, whose life we draw,
Within and over business toils,
Beyond domestic cares and hopes,
There grew another stronger life;
A life of sadness, torturing pain,
Of inward burden for the wronged,
A life that dared to do or die,
To break the chains that others bore.
He came in heart, to stand with Him
Who mother, sister, brother found
Outside of consanguineous tie.

Where Freedom's battle fiercely raged
O'er *Kansas*' fertile plains and vales,
Through blood-stained streets of smoking towns,
'Mid greatest dangers, BROWN was found.
His home was made a burning pile,
His sons were butchered at his side;
But faithful to his Freedom vows,
And strong in consciousness of right,
His iron will and eagle eye
Ne'er failed, nor blanched, nor turned aside,
Till Slavery's hordes were foiled and fled,
And Freedom held the beauteous land.

But inward sorrow deeper grew,
And pain for other hearts in pain.
This pain so strong within him grew,
O'erlapped and folded round his soul,
That life was only gain to him
Which gave release to those in chains;
That praise or blame from men was naught,
And fear of man was swept away.
This pain consumed him like a fire,
And burned away the metes and bounds

Which men have set, of civil right,
And bands of fleeing hunted men,
Had BROWN for steward, leader, guide,
Who brought them safe to Freedom's shore.

Amid *Virginia's* broken wilds,
The Shenandoah takes its rise.
Skirting the mountain's western base,
Past farm-house, village, mills, and towns,
Like thread of silver light it runs,
The pride and beauty of the vale.
In ancient time it massed its strength;
Joining Potomac's rising flood;
They cleft the mountain to its root,
And tore a pathway to the sea.
The walls of rock that reach the sky,
And beetling crags, the story tell.
But Commerce made this pass a road,
And Industry her temples built,
Till at the trysting-place of streams
Sat *Harper's Ferry*, like a gem,
In mountain gray and green incased.

And BROWN, whose soul had mingled moods
Of storm and sunshine, peace and fire,
Saw in those quiet, silvery streams,
And rugged mountains, scarred and torn,
An open door, through which to pierce
The prison walls; and thence to lead
The captives forth, to see the sun,
And breathe the Freedom-sweetened air.

Beneath the shelter of the night
A blow was struck! Historic blow!
'Twas Freedom's first aggressive blow,
And morning light found men in arms
On soil which Slavery sacred held.
A handful only in the band,

But prophecy of countless hosts,
Whose flashing swords and thundering guns
Should leap and blaze, and boom and crash,
Till Slavery should be known no more.
   'Twas here the rubicon was crossed,
The line dividing words and blows.
   Till now each blow was in defense
Of person, land, or civil right,
But this had struck the bastile's doors.

   The blow was heard through all the land.
   The echoes, from the North returned,
In tones of censure, fear, alarm,
Mingled with sympathy and cheer.
   The echoes from the South were filled
With tones of terror, wild affright,
Vindictive bitterness and hate,
A pandemonium Babel scream,
Whose every note defiance breathed,
And cried till hoarse for swift revenge.
   The kings, who rule by right divine,
Their sacred persons none may touch,
Jehovah, their right hand and shield.
   And Slavery had so long been king,
Incense and offering to him given,
That devotees before his throne
Saw, in the challenge of his right,
Both regicide and deicide in one.
   The prison doors' withstood the blow;
The foes of Freedom gathered fast,
And Brown was prisoner in their hands,
While friends and helpers slept in death.

   The cross, once instrument of shame,
By Pilate's act, was glorified,
When Jesus was condemned to die.
   And buried ages nowhere show
A spot so luminous and bright

As shines from Calvary's sacred hill,
By Pilate lifted to the sight
Of men and angels evermore.

JOHN BROWN! he had a felon's death,
But gibbet and the hangman's rope
Were, by the cause for which he died,
Transformed to throne and laurel wreath.
When led from prison forth to die,
There waited humbly by his path,
Slave mother, with her infant child.
His friends were few, no words of cheer,
No prayer or text from sacred priest,
For those whose prayers he loved were far;
But soldiers, with their bayonets set,
Were guarding him on every side.
A cup of water freely given,
Shall ever meet its just reward.
One voice of kindness reached his ear,
It came from lips enslaved: "Old man,
I wish that I could give you help."
The prisoner paused. He stooped and kissed
The babe, borne in its mother's arms,
The seal of love. It never failed,
He loved his own unto the end.

Rebellion, treason, civil war,
Are words familiar to our ears.
Vast holocausts of human life,
At Moloch's bloody shrine were laid,
When Slavery and her viperous brood
Incited treason in the land.
Her captains met no felon's death!
JOHN BROWN alone for treason tried,
By hands of common hangman died;
But when those captains are forgot,
Freemen shall throng the sacred spot,
The granite shaft shall pierce the sky,

Where Freedom's martyr came to die;
And picture, statue, poet's song,
From age to age, his fame prolong.
His body molders in the grave,
His deathless spirit marches on.

XI.
DIVINE METHODS OF EARTHLY GOVERNMENT.

LAW is the utterance of a voice
  Whose pulses fill the universe,
  The robe which, in its ample fold,
Doth atom and archangel hold,
And through its awful grooves doth run
The power that holds in place the sun,
While reaching through the spaces far
It molds and measures every star,
And balances, with nice design,
The myriads marshaled in its line;
Spirit and matter, at its word,
Their pathways keep around their LORD;
Each atom, planet, moving force,
With suns and systems in their course,
Ne'er swerving from appointed way
While sweeping through eternity.
  Men build with care, foundations lay,
With brace and girder for their stay,
With plumb and level shape each course,
To stand secure 'mid every force.
  And when Niagara they would span,
Or cities join by iron strand,
Their cable's *termini* they key
'Neath pyramids of masonry.
  But He who builds the worlds of light,
Which beautify and crown the night,
And sends them on their golden race,

Whose circuits reach through endless space,
Uses no brace or iron band
To join to His almighty hand;
On nothing hangs celestial balls
Which gild and grace ethereal halls.

   All powers, perfections, burning flames,
Bearing their high exalted names,
Matter and mind before Him wait,
With LAW, his minister of state.

   Matter is passive, never asks
Relief from its appointed tasks;
Submissive still, it ne'er complains,
Nor chafes against its binding chains.
   Mind, gifted with internal force,
By inward power doth choose its course;
Unlike the ship which spreads its sail
Where winds and tides her course prevail,
But like the power by fire-breath born,
Mind cleaves its way through wind and storm.

   But ships, by inward force propelled,
From day to day must bearing take.
   And mind but yesterday new-formed
Needs shape its course by higher lights.
   The bowsprit lantern, hanging free,
When followed 'lone may only guide
To endless circles on the sea,
Or lead the way to dangerous reefs,
Or sunken rocks of wild despair.

   The lights above, the sun and stars
High o'er the mists and fogs of earth,
Forever shining from their place,
Are guides for men; observed with care,
We safely make the destined port.

Abandoned these, then passing drift
May drive us on the hidden rocks,
And make our being total wreck.

These lights above, that night and day
Go flaming their celestial way,
Contending none for higher place,
And no collisions in their race,
Examples give to men below,
Each in appointed way to go,
Brother with brother ne'er collide,
But kindly journey side by side.
  Alas for us! these lessons high,
Forever shining from the sky,
And words divine ELOHIM spoke
By human will were quickly broke;
And now, by angry passions tossed,
And each by each their orbits crossed,
They jar, collide, impinge, destroy,
Thus wrecking each the other's joy.

A world was made. Created fair,
And hung in equipoise on high,
Joined to its glorious central sun,
Kissed lovingly with roseate light,
A new-bloomed flower of the sky,
Shedding its starry fragrance forth;
It took its place within the whirl
Of dancing spheres, and joined its song
With constellations hymning praise.
  Ten thousand, thousand, thousand years,
Both in and out, and round and round,
It kept its place and trilled its song,
A joyous wanderer of the sky.
  While passing near the utmost verge
Of vast Creation's boundary line,
Rounding the curve that turns again,
From depth and darkness yet unknown,

Toward cultivated fields of light,
It broke the bands of rightful law,
And, flying from its traveled track,
Swift over precipice it went.
 Beyond domain of law, beyond
Where heat and light and life are known,
Through dark abysmal space it flew,
No power to check its onward way.
 The utter nothing which it passed
Gave back no sound, and took no trace;
But aimless, shoreless, starless, all,
The world which once was wondrous fair
Went down, and out, was lost nowhere.
 Thus soul of man, by law unkept,
Doth wander to eternal night;
And guiding hand of law unclasped,
The universe would chaos prove.

 Civilization! pregnant term,
Including science, culture, art,
The pen, the press, the electric wire,
The home, the school, the church, the state,
Asylum, hospital, retreat,
Wisdom and kindness, truth and love,
With all that lifts from savagery,
Is closer harmony with law.
 Its fullness, length, and breadth, and height,
Encompasses, surrounds, and fills
All claims, relations, duties, needs
Of man. And in the golden age,
Which sages hope and poets dream,
When truth and love shall fill the earth,
That brighter, better, happier time
Shall be completer reign of law.
 And in the holy blessed clime
Which faith beholds beyond the veil,
The fullness of its joys shall be
Divine and human harmony.

Two instruments JEHOVAH hath
To curb and guide man's erring feet,—
The proclamation of his word,
And sword of civil government.
These, free and healthful in their work,
According with Eternal law,
Earth is preserved from social wreck.

Holy Bible! book of truth,
Containing wondrous history:
Creation's record, birth of time,
The infant race, advent of sin,
The first-born child a murderer;
Antagonistic good and ill,
Growing corruption, judgment flood;
The ark, salvation, earth renewed,
Increase, dispersion, strife, and war;
The chosen seed, bondage severe,
Deliverance, safety, shouts, and songs;
Sinai's mountain top of flame,
With thunders, voices words of law;
Rebellion, discords, unbelief,
Water from rocks, and heavenly bread;
Pillar of fire; the ark of God,
And temple courts from pattern built,
And holy place within the veil—
SHEKINAH's earthly resting-place;
With Joshua, judges, priests, and kings,
And songs of wisdom, praise, and prayer—
Elijah's prayer, and falling fire,
Isaiah's rapt and burning words,
A weeping prophet's warning voice,
Ezekiel's wheels and eyes of flame,
And Chebar's lonely captives' wail,
With lions harmless, fires made void;
Nineveh, Persia, Babylon,
Damascus, Egypt, Greece, and Rome;
Through nations wide and ages long,

O'er Pharaoh's, Xerxes', Cæsar's thrones,
The providential plowshare passed,
Crumbling their dynasties,—
Preparing earth for seed of truth,
Whose fruit shall shake like Lebanon.

And through these ages, passing slow,
By God's anointed ones was given
The wondrous book; archives of earth,
And to our sight revealing worlds,
Eternal and invisible.

By hand divine the threads were drawn
O'er empires, mountains, shores, and seas,
And stretching through the centuries;
Then through this warp was interwove
Amazing facts of God, revealed;
His birth, his life, his tragic death,
His resurrection, crowning proof
Of Prince of life, in death despoiled.
 These truths divine so interwove,
On background of historic page,
Their facts can never be denied
Till men reverse the centuries' flow,
Or earthly annals blot from sight.
 While clear and bright, majestic, strong,
In matchless beauty, wisdom, grace,
The lineaments of Jesus shine,
And human power can ne'er destroy
The wondrous picture shining there.

This gift of God, this light divine,
Is book of statutes, judgments, claims,
Pertaining to the present life,
And reaching to the life to come.
 These precepts touch on every side,
The child and parent, husband, wife,

And throw the ægis of their power
O'er self and home and social life,
Including every land and race.

To speak this word of God abroad
Declaring plain, "Thus saith the Lord,"
As highest sanction truth can have,
This is the preacher's special work.
The word may flow from honeyed lips,
And posture, manner, diction, voice,
May all combine to charm the sense;
While learning, logic, mental force,
May help complete the preacher's power.
But this is only empty air,
That comes and goes with passing breath,
A tinkling cymbal, sounding brass,
A tone from reed or quivering string,
Till founded on "Thus saith the Lord."
This fulcrum fixed, the word becomes
A hammer, breaking granite rocks,
Or Roman catapult, the wall,
A sword, dividing bone from bone,
Through joint and marrow finding way,
A tongue of flame, a burning fire.

The chosen ones whom God appoints,
Have only right the word to speak;
No penalties can they inflict,
No dungeons, fagots, ax, or sword,
No inquisition's darkened cells,
Where torture is a science taught,
And pain is measured, grain by grain,
To physic maladies of soul;
No right to use the temporal arm,
Mandates t' enforce on recreant ones.
By word of truth, divinely given,
The conscience only may they touch,
And quick'ning dormant moral sense,

Affections elevate and cleanse ;
Lifting the soul to higher life.

The second gracious instrument,
Ordained of God for human weal,
Is gift of civil government.
The highest function of these powers
Is to interpret and declare,
And wisely to man's needs apply,
Supreme and universal law.
With righteous statutes duly framed,
And scales of justice even set,
Ne'er turned from proper poise by gold,
But balanced only by the truth,
The civil law is hymn of praise,
An anthem welcome in the skies.

In wild, anarchic, boastful times,
Vain kings and proud democracies,
May claim the authorship of law.
But tides will rise, and seasons roll,
Though Canute strive to stay the sea,
Or France enthrone philosophy.
No league of earthly potentates,
Or rulers' counsel 'gainst the Lord,
To break his bands, or loose his cords,
Shall overthrow eternal laws.
Let kings and judges of the earth
Instruction hear, and serve the Lord,
Before the iron rod shall fall
And dash their schemes like potter's wares.

Pretended plenipotents of heaven,
Claiming commissions from the skies,
Who seek to place the seal divine
On laws opposed to righteousness—
Blind leaders of a people blind—
Shall fall together in the pit.

When kings and prophets thus unite
To bend eternal right to wrong,
And sin enthrone in place of God,
Then earth's foundations seem to shake.

But driving in the skirmish lines,
Does not o'erwhelm the solid ranks,
And oft, when outer works are scaled,
The range of heavier fire is reached.
And in the magazines of God,
The scourges of a guilty land,
Exhaustless, still his orders wait:
War! with his feet of blood and fire
Trampling in anger through the land;
Gaunt Famine! with his sharpened teeth,
Hunting his prey with hungry eyes;
And Pestilence! whose fetid breath
Poisons the victims of her kiss.
And when God's ministries of grace,
Are turned against his righteous laws,
He pours the vials of his wrath.

Elijah, prince of Hebrew seers,
From Tishbe came; the Jordan crossed,
Ascending slow Samaria's hill,
He stood uncalled in Ahab's courts.
Baal and Ashtaroth were there,
Temples and groves to Venus reared,
Zidonian gods of hateful name,
Whom Jezebel to Israel brought;
Jehovah's altars nowhere seen.
And impious Ahab mocking said:
"See how the word of Moses fails,
Israel hath turned to idol gods,
And still the heavens give their rain."
Elijah spake: "As God doth live,
No dew nor rain shall bless this land,
Except according to my word."

And years passed on: the ground was burned;
The pools were dried ; the flocks and herds
Stood famishing and snuffed the wind ;
While messengers of Ahab sought,
Unceasing, for the prophet's life,
As one that troubled Israel.
But none cut down the idol groves,
And none Jehovah's altars built.

Again the prophet met the king,
And soon on Carmel's heights were seen,
Prophets of Baal and of groves,
Reaching nine hundred and fifty men;
While of Jehovah's prophets there
One man, Elijah, stood alone,
Waiting the answering fire from heaven.
The fire fell. The people cried:
"Jehovah! he is God alone ;
The priests of Baal all shall die."
Again the prophet bowed in prayer,
And from the skies the answering showers
Flooded the parched and barren earth.

But still the king relented not,
And still the sacrifices smoked
On altars reared to idol gods.
And Jezebel, intoxicate
With power and lust, with Ahab joined
To crush Jehovah's worshipers.
Thus law enthroned the powers of wrong,
And force drove out God's messengers.
A cave on Horeb's awful mount
Became the prophet's hiding place.

While waiting thus there came a voice,
Which asked: "Elijah, why thou here?"
The prophet in his anguish cried:
"Thy children have forsaken thee,

Thy holy covenant they have broke,
Thine altars have been overthrown,
Thy prophets with the sword are slain,
And only I am left. And me
They seek, to take my life away."
　The voice replied : "Go forth and stand
Upon the mount before the Lord,
And earthquake, wind, and fire, and voice,
Shall show God ruleth still the earth ;
Then hence away ; this message take:
Hazael anoint for Syria's king,
And Jehu Israel's king shall be,
Elisha prophet in thy room.
　Him that escapes from Hazael's sword,
The sword of Jehu shall lay low,
And those whom Jehu fails to kill,
Elisha with his sword shall slay,
Till idol altars, priests, and groves,
No longer shall the land pollute."
　The sword was quickly bathed in blood,
And Ahab's blood was lapped by dogs,
While Jezebel the dogs did eat,
And with the besom of His wrath,
God swept the land that thrust Him out.

　All soldiers would their captains crown,
And Christian soldiers longed to see
The Gospel, with its tongue of fire,
Melting away the bondman's chains;
And in all nations' wondering sight,
To place this crown on Jesus' brow.
　Our eyes were veiled, we did not see,
That first the "King of righteousness,"
And after that the "King of peace."

O'er all the lands by bondmen trod,
The civil law, by God designed,
Defense and shelter for the weak,

Was made the instrument to forge
And closely rivet Slavery's chains;
And prophets of the Holy One
Were asked to place their Master's seal
Upon these covenants of crime.
  When harp and flute and dulcimer
Their music joined, all men must bow,
Or fuel be for furnace fires.
  And most unto this image bowed;
The remnant martyrs fell, or fled
As exiles from the guilty land.

  All seemed secure, and Slavery thought
The courts of heaven were subsidized,
The Eternal One was leagued with sin.

XII.

OPENING OF THE ARMED CONFLICT.

HAIL, beauteous sunshine! joy of earth,
Pouring in molten glory forth,
Flowing from that exhaustless urn
Where thoughts divine to sunlight turn.
Hail, balmy air! o'er earth outspread,
Sleeping in quiet 'bove our head,
Or joined with light, through golden day
The zephyrs gently round us play.
Hail, robes of beauty! from the sod
Lifting aloft their praise to God;
With earth, and sky, and light, and air,
Balanced by strange electric fire,
Without alarm we safely rest,
Like birdling sheltered in its nest.

Anon the subtle ceaseless force,
Disturbed and varied in its course,
The darkened portents fill the sky,
And warring winds around us fly;
The lightnings flash athwart the gloom,
And thunders peal the day of doom;
Tornadoes sweep along the plain,
With death and ruin in their train;
And storms depict the wrath divine,
As mercy doth in sunlight shine.

The years of sunshine swift had passed,
When Freedom's spirit walked the earth,

And rugged labor, strong and true,
Sustained by her inspiring breath,
Had changed the wilderness to bloom;
And cities grew beside the seas,
And white-winged rovers plowed the deep,
While joy and plenty filled the land.
   A generation now had come
To whom the dread alarm of war
Seemed like the ages long ago,
Forever buried from our sight.
   And many thought our purer age
Had passed those dread barbaric times
When wholesale murder history stained.

   But clouds were gathering in the sky,
And winds of discord fiercely blew,
Precursors of a coming storm.
   The thickly gathering mists and gloom
November norther failed to clear;
And through the weary winter months
Darkness and terror moved apace,
While pain was wringing every joint,
And horror creeping through the nerves.
   Grim shapes of evil stalked abroad,
And jangling Discord's babel sounds
Were breaking on the saddened air.

   One burst of sunlight briefly shone;
The troubled nation's chosen chief
Stood at the threshold of his work.
   His voice pronounced the solemn oath,
His lips had touched the holy book,
In tenderness his words went forth,
To touch the sweeter angel chords
Of hearts now moved by bitter strife.
   He spoke of country, home, and peace,
Of hearth-stones bound by kindred ties,
And hopes that centered in this land.

One moment, and the sunlight passed;
The dark storm-clouds o'erspread the sky,
Their edges tinged with lurid flame.

On *Carolina's* eastern coast
An inlet from the seas is found,
Land-locked and sheltered from the blasts,
A beauteous, spacious haven lies.
Two streams which from the mountains flow
Mingle their waters at its head.
Between these rivers *Charleston* lies,
Like precious gem on beauty's hand,
Kept in its place by golden clasps.
Within this harbor *Sumter* stands:
Built by the nation's lavished wealth,
Held by the nation's trusted guards,
Crowned by the nation's flag of stars,
It stood, a symbol of her power,
Keeping this gate-way of the land,
Bidding defiance to her foes,
Sheltering the city at its side.

South Carolina's fiery zeal
Had sought to break the golden band
Which bound her to her sister States;
To pluck her shining silver star
From out the nation's field of blue;
To tear our country's flag in twain,
And 'neath its tattered fragments hide
The vileness of their cherished crime.
This fatal frenzy swiftly spread,
State after State her footsteps trod,
Straight to the foaming gulf of fire.

Imbecile weakness held the place
Whence leaping forth, in day of yore,
A JACKSON's blazing, trenchant words,
Blasted their budding treason schemes.

And over all our southern land,
From court-house, hall, and ship, and fort,
Our glory was pulled down in shame,
And in its place was raised on high
The bars to keep our land in twain.

Still *Sumter* stood, unchanged, alone.
Bearing her country's flag of stars,
In number, station, brightness, all,
No stain upon its azure field.
The morning sun kissed first its folds,
When rising from his ocean bed.
Its waving glory midday cheered.
There evening sunshine lingered long,
Charmed with its radiant, dazzling hues.
And starry splendors of the night
Gazed gladly from their wondrous height,
While through the silent midnight hour
Unto this flaming, floating flower
The whispering winds were murmuring sweet,
As lovers oft their vows repeat.

And longing, tear-wet, anxious eyes,
From all the nation's wide domain,
Were resting on its shining folds,
While lands afar beyond the sea
With variant feelings watched and prayed.
The oppressor wished it drowned in shame,
With all its glorious memories lost.
The burdened, struggling ones beheld
The symbol of the people's right,
And prayed that it might ever float.

The weaklings, in the place of power,
Forbade all acts of self-defense,
While day by day, on every side,
Was planted enginery of war,
Until the iron wall was built

From which to pour the streams of fire
On those who served the nation's flag.
  Still in its center *Sumter* stood,
Bearing aloft its flág of stars,
While loyal hearts both brave and true,
Led by the gallant ANDERSON,
Though starved, and hopeless of relief,
Refused to yield to treason's sway.

  The April ides were passing by,
And in the sunny southern clime
The buds were bursting into bloom.
  Through all the silent wintry months,
In secret chambers, nature wrought
To ornament her spring attire;
And leaf and lichen, flower and fern,
Were tucked and plaited, frilled and fringed,
Shaded and draped, symmetric all,
And odorous with sweet perfume,
Till earth was clothed in virgin robes,
And Eden seemed returned again.
  The lambs were racing o'er the fields,
Telling the bliss of conscious life.
  The birds were spending honeymoon,
With songs and plumage fresh and new.
  The god of day, in regal state,
Had sent his flaming heralds forth
To lift the curtains of the night,
And sprinkle light o'er eastern sky
Before his golden chariot wheels;
And earth, expectant, saw approach
Her lord and king, who day by day
Repeats creation's miracle.

  While earth and sky thus wait the day,
A signal from the treason chiefs
Kindles that iron wall to flame.
  And over *Sumter's* turrets strong,

And 'gainst her frowning granite walls,
On red and white her banner bore
There poured a molten stream of fire.
  The sulphurous smoke obscured the sky;
It lifted up its darkening folds,
Defiant to the midday sun.
  It spread o'er earth like funeral pall,
Enshrouding all that men hold dear.
  It rolled o'er bay and shore and town,
Bearing the spores from whence should spring
Harvests of ruin, fields of fire.

  The winds and lightnings bore the sound
Of that first boom of angry war
To every hearth-stone of the land.
  It rolled along the Atlantic shore,
And echoed back from *Plymouth Rock*.
  It scaled the Alleghany's heights,
And floated o'er the inland seas.
  The mighty Mississippi heard
The awful cadence of that voice,
Which burdened all its vales and plains.
  Among the Rocky Mountain peaks
Endless reverberations rolled,
And on and on, o'er Sierra's crests,
Through *California's* vine-clad fields,
Till mingled with the ocean's roar.
  The mighty chieftains of the press,
They heard the crash of hostile arms,
And their great trumpets, million voiced,
Waked every echo of the land.
  Commerce, affrighted, held her breath,
And paleness overspread her face.
  The bankers' granite money vaults,
Though strongly built and safely locked,
They heard the awful din abroad,
And trembled for their hoarded gold;
While Wall Street felt a shivering chill,

Precursor of the fever's rage,
When wild, delirious fancies rule.
  And wives were frantic in their fears,
And sisters o'er their brothers wept,
While mothers on their stalwart sons
With anguish gazed, and clasped their babes,
Thankful to hold them in their arms.
  The sound rolled through the ocean deeps,
'Twas heard distinct in kingly courts,
And echoed through the marts of trade
In Europe's ancient capitals.
  The prophets of the subject race,
Who long had gazed through dark and gloom,
For harbingers of Freedom's dawn,
They heard the sound. And in their eyes
A gleam of light like sunshine blazed.
  They knew the Hand divine could guide
The conflagration, kindling now;
That winds and storms obey His will,
And at His breath their iron chains,
As flax in fire, could ashes turn.

  The storied banner of the free
Received anew a fiery chrism,
Fresh poured from fratricidal hands,
Prophetic of a thousand fields,
Where, 'mid the battle's burning blaze,
Begrimed with smoke and torn with shells,
Its stripes and stars should bow in shame,
Or float in victory o'er its foes.

  The soldiers faced this storm of fire
Till *Sumter* was a smoldering pile;
Until the haughty treason chiefs
Beheld the struggle drawing nigh,
Whose mighty throes would shake the earth,
And wrap a continent in flame,

Before a single shining star
Should fade from out its heaven of blue.
   And then, with sad and reverent air,
With tearful eye and tender touch,
They furled the banner of their love,
Bearing it northward o'er the seas,
Till loving hands, in future days,
Should lift it to its place again.

XIII.

HORRORS AND SORROWS OF WAR.

TWO thousand miles of battle line,
Three thousand thousand men in arms,
Ten thousand thundering cannons roar,
The scream and thud of bursting shells,
And bullets like the falling rain,
The mountain tops enwreathed in smoke,
The vales illumed by burning towns,
Rivers by fiery monsters trod,
With breath of flame and sting of death.
  The rush and roar of rolling wheels,
The creak and crash of wagon trains,
The stretchers hastening to the rear,
And surgeons with the saw and knife.
  Broken and crushed and bleeding forms,
And sickness wasting day by day.
  The prisoners starving in their pens,
And longing, with their hungry eyes,
For sight of home and friends again;
And open graves on every side,
Where nameless thousands lie unknown.
  The varying fortunes of the field,
With lines, now broken here and there,
Then closed again with piles of slain.
  Now sheltered by the heaped-up earth,
Now water-soaked in rifle pits,
Now delving underneath the fort,
Now blown in air by bursting mine.

These are of war the indices,
Whose powers no human thought can reach.
  Through flowery spring and summer heat,
Autumnal beauty, winter's frost,
Four dreadful years this work went on,
From opening of these judgment seals,
Filling the land with direst woe.

  O! hateful, horrid, hellish war!
What pen can paint thy visage dark?
What tongue can tell thy awful curse?
  Olla podrida, dark and deep,
Where every passion possible
To fallen man tumultuous boils.
  Where spirits black and blue and gray
Come bringing all the poisoned drugs,
Compounded by their devilish art,
With gibe and flaunt, and sneer and curse,
With maudlin, beastly orgies,
And gibbering incantations wild,
Their hell-broth brew; then ladle out
To smirch and poison living men.
  The glory, rising from the same,
Is but a flame-lit lurid sky
From fire-doomed city in the night,
Where clearer light of opening day
Shows ruin in its blackened path.

  Yet flitting through this storm of wrath
Are seen the gleam of angels' wings;
And through the black and stifling smoke
Are shining holy, pitying eyes;
And tender, helping, loving hands
Are pouring balm on bleeding wounds,
And binding up worse broken hearts.

  Beneath a vaulted roof of light,
Stretching afar on either hand,

The wonder of admiring crowds
Gathered from all the tribes of earth,
Briarius, modern monster, stands.
　Within that molded organism,
Lifting its awful form on high,
An iron net-work of design,
A spirit dwells, invisible
To mortal sight; and only known
By going forth of matchless force.
　His inspirations thrill his frame,
His heart-beats lift his iron arms,
His shoulders press their iron gears,
And power, unmeasured power, appears.

　He stretches forth his hundred hands,
And touches with his finger tips
The work intrusted to his care.
　One hand is breaking granite rocks,
And sifting out their golden sands.
　Another clasps the dampened sheet,
And drops therefrom the printed page.
　The bar of steel is drawn and rolled,
And fashioned for its destined use.
　One little finger deftly thrust
Through solid massive iron bars.
　Another making needles' eyes,
Or polishing their sharpened points.
　Some weave the golden tapestry,
Dropping each shining thread in place,
Till pictures bright as morning light,
And beauteous as the starry night,
Are fashioned from the shimmering floss.
　One hand can dredge the river's bed,
Another spin the gossamer,
Flowing in beauty's bridal veil.
　Thus God-like will, one single force
Is cleft, and multiplied, until
Ten thousand fingers move at once.

And thus that awful complex form,
Through which goes forth a nation's might,
Is wrought into organic life,
From fire and steel and living men.
 Its giant corps are living arms,
Its grand divisions mighty hands;
Fingers, brigades and regiments;
Iron and brass are bones and joints,
And horsemen mailed its tendons are.
 Soldiers are nerve-points, set in line,
The scouts and spies are eyes and ears,
Through which the silent soul, within,
Surveys the movements of his foes.
 One single will controls the whole.

 He reaches out his giant arms,
Clasping his enemies therein,
And anaconda-like, attempts
To crush them in his tight'ning folds.
 He masses nerve and joint and bone,
With which to strike the potent blow,
To break opposing iron walls.
 Sometimes his bleeding hand recoils,
Shattered and broken in the strife.
 Again opposing arms are locked,
Like antlers of the warring deer,
While fruitless struggles waste their strength,
Till each is glad to 'scape its foe.
 These struggling giants shake the earth,
Their vaporous sweat obscures the sky,
And seems to threaten sun and stars.

 An army, formed for dress parade,
Its banners floating on the breeze,
Its even lines of flashing steel,
Its columns moving like a wall,
Or forming geometric squares,
Complete as Euclid's theorems,

While music, motion, dress, and arms,
Join to complete their glittering charms,
Is picture, glowing, fresh, and bright.

But when the hour of battle comes,
And howling wolves, of pain and death,
Make bare their sharpened bloody fangs;
When storm-clouds black make night of noon,
And bursting jets of sulphurous flame,
Are spouting from the troubled earth,
Precursors of the earthquake's tread;
And mountains belching streams of fire;
Then play-day pomp, and trumpets' blare,
Like morning mists, dissolve in air.
When through the hurtling iron rain,
The columns of contending hosts
Press forward to the battle shock,
With thunder crash like day of doom;
Then broken ranks, begrimed and foul,
The corpse-strewn field, the new-made graves,
No more is picture, clean and bright,
But powder-stained and soaked in blood,
And torn and trampled in the mire.

But horrors of the battle-field
Are not alone the scourge of war.
 The shot that took a mortal life
Has broken many loving hearts,
Far from the bloody fields of strife.
 Not only Israel's shepherd king
Has cried in anguish o'er his slain:
 "O Absalom! my son! my son!"
But sorrows which no pen has traced,
Ten thousand fathers' hearts have borne.
 And Rachels, weeping for their dead,
Are not confined to Ramah's fields,
But swords which drank the blood of sons
The souls of mothers also pierced.

And homes which dotted mountain side,
From sunlight felt a strange eclipse,
When tidings came from fields of death.
　The widow gazed on little ones,
With air distraught and pallid cheek,
Reaching afar her weary arms
Empty and hungry for the dead.

　And pensive maiden slowly walked
At twilight hour, in lonely vale,
Brooding in silence o'er her woes.
　That vale, so late by joy illumed,
As lover's vows were falling sweet
Into her waiting, willing ears,
And ruby lips received the seal
Of honored, truthful, human love,
Where birds and bees, and whispering leaves,
Of love's sweet vows were witnesses.
　Alone she held her secret joy,
And now alone must bear the pain;
While he, whose love her life did crown,
Now sleeps afar in nameless grave.

　And doors of marble palaces,
Where lions crouched on granite steps,
Had golden handles draped in crape;
While waited, hushed and sad within,
A stricken group. Through crowded streets
The long procession slowly passed,
With muffled drum and funeral dirge.
　Horses and grooms were draped in black,
And tossing plumes were looking down,
Where rosewood, silver, satin, joined
To make luxurious sleeping-couch
For him, who thus from war returned,
Wrapped in the nation's flag of stars.
　The master of these stately halls,

From months of absence coming now,
No greetings gave to wife or child.
  A thousand tongues his triumphs told,
The silver stars his shoulders graced,
But silence on his lips was pressed,
And hands were folded on his breast.
  The crowds are gone, the parlors closed,
The dead is there and nameless woe.

  And living ones, the war o'erpast,
Return to meet the loved of old,
With broken forms and ruined health;
Or worse than sickness, wounds, or death,
Some who went forth in youthful bloom,
From homes of prayer and innocence,
Return, sin-poisoned, and despoiled,
And shame to those they once rejoiced.

  Converging lines of solar light
Kindle the place they touch to flame.
  Composite forces reach the stars,
And lead them forth through endless space,
Their winding pathways ever new.
  Motives are mingled, guiding men,
And sometimes high and pure and true
Are re-enforced by others base.
  The streams, which fill the river's bank,
Have many springs among the hills,
And often adverse courses flow;
Till turned by unseen hands, they glide
Into the mighty stream, that bears
A nation's commerce on its tides.

  Thus motives, wide as pole from pole,
And forces, variant in their aims,
In war's hot crucible were fused,
And by supernal powers poured out

To Slavery kill, both root and branch,
And wash the land with streams of fire.
  The hoping, restless, feverish youth,
Anxious to see the world afar;
The man, whose life was stained with crime,
Who wished to hide from watching eyes,
Or sought to cleanse a sullied name,
Saw here his opportunity.
  And men, who had a greed of gold,
Believed their harvest time had come.
  Ambitious ones, who wished to pave
Their way to place of civil trust,
Or sought to win an honored name,
On shining roll of human fame.
  And patriot ones, who kept enshrined,
Within their inmost hearts, their love
For country dearer than their life,
As Israel kept the ark of God
Within the holiest of all;
Sons of the noble sires who built
A temple here for human rights,
And hid, within its sacred courts,
Diviner truths than earth had known,
Which in time's fullness should go forth
In blessing to each race and age;
They trembled for the sacred ark,
And hastened to confront its foes.
  And wildest abolitionists,
Of all men most impracticable,
Who never thought as others thought;
Who cried in times of war for peace;
Who union called a league with hell;
When war's black shadow filled the land,
Forgot their peaceful note to pipe,
And ceased to rail 'gainst union bonds.
  And earnest, prayerful, Christian men,
Who, self-surrend'ring, bowed to Him
Whose advent song was peace on earth,

They read the word of God anew,
And found he also brought a sword.
　And thus, beneath the upas-tree,
The ax was laid, and every force,
Angels and devils, each unchanged,
Were joined to strike the awful blow,
To cut and cast it into the fire.

XIV.

PREPARATION OF INSTRUMENTS FOR THE WORK.

AN acorn dropped upon the earth,
A breath of wind was wandering by,
Which caught some withered falling leaves
And piled them o'er the fallen seed.
 The rains of autumn drenched its bed,
And 'neath the winter frosts and snows
It lay unnoticed and unknown.
 When spring came roaming o'er the hills,
Peering within sequestered nooks
For violets and forget-me-nots,
She spied beneath the withered leaves
This modest amber forest gem—
A polished cone on cupule base—
And with its quiet beauty charmed,
She breathed thereon her loving breath.
 The warm embrace of loving spring
Sent through its heart a secret joy,
And stirred its slumbering powers to life.
 It first sent out a thread-like lip,
To reach the breast of mother earth.
 It then threw off its horny cap,
And opening wide its fruit-filled hands,
Forth from the inmost soul there came,
Seeking the light, a tiny stalk.

 Then light and air and earth and sea,

With rich profusion, brought their gifts;
And wrought to build a tapering stem,
And cover it with leafy crown.
  And while the years went flowing by,
The golden sunshine, dews, and showers,
The winter frosts and wrestling storms,
Each in their turn had clasped and kissed
This growing monarch of the hills,
Until its crown embraced the sky,
Its mighty arms were reached afar,
And battling with tornado blasts
It keyed its roots among the rocks;
And limbs grew cords of braided wire,
Till every ligneous thread was drawn
And twisted to its utmost strength.

  And when this monarch of the wood
Became the keel of mammoth ship,
And all its gnarled and twisted limbs
Were wrought into her rounded sides,
She then withstood the wind's wild play,
And walked unharmed o'er mountain waves;
She trod the fields of frozen ice,
And struck unbroke on rocky shore.

  Thus is the grain of timber wrought,
Selected for severest tests;
And from the secret chambers come
Great actors in our real life.

  A basket floated on the Nile
In which there slept an infant child;
No earthly parentage was known,
But seemingly cast out to die.
  A princess walked the river's banks,
And from the waters Moses drew.
  That child, so helpless and unknown,

Was trained to do the greatest work
That e'er was done by human hands.
  At feet of sages he was taught
All that Egyptian wisdom knew.
  As prince in Pharaoh's storied courts,
He learned the arts of kingly rule.
  As captain in his mighty hosts,
He learned the ancient warrior's trade,
And methods of the field and camp.
  At forty years of age he stood
The foremost man of all his time.

  When test of moral fiber came,
Then faithful to his fathers' God,
And to his suffering kinsmen true,
He turned away from courts and kings,
And fled to Midian's pathless wilds.

  And in those awful solitudes,
'Mid trees and rocks and mountain peaks,
And babbling streams and grassy glades,
With bleat of lambs and song of birds,
And human love of wife and child,
With nature he communion held.
  Adoring there the holy One,
And gazing on his mighty works,
He fed within the hallowed fires
Of truth and love and holiness.
  And rising suns and rolling years
Swept onward like the river tide,
Till forty added years had flown;
While he unconscious still remained,
Waiting the work by God ordained.

  A burning bush! still unconsumed,
A voice that had no lip or breath,
And Horeb's wandering exile heard
The summons to a wondrous life.

Henceforth Jehovah's legate sent
To proud, oppressive Pharaoh's court.
Henceforth God's minister of wrath,
In plagues of darkness, storms, and death.
Henceforth commander of the host,
Who from Egyptian bondage fled.
Henceforth on Sinai's flame-fringed mount,
To hear again that awful voice,
First heard in Horeb's burning bush,
And see Jehovah face to face;
Receiving from his fleshless hands
The sacred stones his fingers traced.
Henceforth to frame a code of laws,
So wise, beneficent, and just,
That all the wide-spread lands of earth,
And all the centuries of time,
Should ever from these fountains draw.
From patterns furnished to prepare
The channels, where henceforth should flow
From sinful man to holy One,
In streaming blood and smoke and fire,
The griefs and groans, the prayers and songs,
Of guilty, sorrowing, hoping souls;
Until these channels, cleansed by blood
Which never human guilt had known,
Should make an open way to God
For all our lost apostate race.
And then from Nebo's glittering peak,
Beholding far the promised land,
Those eyes, which ne'er before were dimmed
When wearied with their earthly gaze,
Saw rise before their gladdened sight
The city of eternal light.

ABRAHAM LINCOLN! forest child,
Of humble parentage the fruit,
Cradled among the mountains wild,
Trod early rugged paths in life.

Save those who walked the virgin earth,
Fresh blooming in Creation's morn,
Each human life has ever been
The product of converging streams.
   Some streams from crystal fountains flowed,
And some had birth in dark morass,
Some tumbling came from mountain heights,
Some sluggish moved through putrid vales,
And in life's wondrous alchemy
The clean and sweet, the turbid, dark,
Each gave a touch, a tinge, a stain
To moving currents of the soul.
   The streams which flow alluvial plains,
Bear onward through the centuries
The foulness gathered in their course;
While those which dash o'er cataracts,
And wind their way through rocky glens,
Or o'er the shingly beaches sing,
Through contact with the earth and air,
Are from their poisonous fetors cleansed.
   And in the lonely forest wilds,
Where rank and riches prestige lose,
And common struggles closely bind
Each near to Nature's throbbing heart;
Distempers of the social life,
And vicious habits in the blood,
Are healed by virtue of her touch,
And streams of life grow pure again.

   Thus LINCOLN's birth and early years
Were shaded by the forest scenes.
   His life, through its paternal stream,
Had mingled with it Quaker blood.
   It gave him plain and simple speech,
A quick, unerring sense of right,
And reverent, humble fear of God.
   His school was hard continuous toil.

His problems were to win his bread
From a reluctant wilderness.
His prizes were the prostrate woods,
And sunshine gleams on rip'ning corn.
His recreations, hunting tours,
Where profit with his pleasure joined.
His *Saratogas*, foreign scenes,
Were flat-boat rides to *New Orleans*,
And foot-sore travel in return.

And in this rugged training-school,
Alert, reliant, he became.
He learned occasion quick to seize,
To lift the rolling log in place,
And boat into the current guide
Without a written precedent.
Among the sinuous mountain paths,
And labyrinth of dangerous wilds,
To look aloft for guiding lights.

One day ne'er built imperial Rome,
Nor set the pyramids in place.
Foundation stones are slowly laid,
On which the towering pile is built.
The roots of mighty ancient trees
Are deeply hid beneath the ground.
And thus, secure from human gaze,
Were laid the massive granite rocks
On which a LINCOLN's life was built.

Advancing manhood contact gave
With men and books and public life,
In courts and legislative halls.
And careful study of the past
Unrolled to his inquiring gaze
Historic nations in their dawn,
Their midday grandeur, and decline.
His careful, philosophic thought

Laid bare the fountains of their life,
And traced the secret poisoned spring
From whence decay and death had flowed.
 He looked beneath the surface veil
Which kindly shades our human life
To learn the needs and drift of men,
And saw the grand design of God
Was universal brotherhood.
 And true to justice, true to right,
To manhood, reason, conscience true,
He won and wore the sobriquet
Of "Honest Abe," and "Uncle Abe."
 The first revealed the public trust,
The latter showed the people's love.
 In person, tall and spare and plain;
In manner, awkward, unrefined.
 In spirit—surface—jovial, light,
O'erflowing with his stories droll,
The bearded froth of dashing wave;
Its depth—majestic, solemn, sweet,
Tender as woman's love, and strong
As ribs of mountain rock, and pure
As ocean deeps or skies of blue.
 Conscious of strength, yet unconsumed
By mad ambition's restless fires;
Sagacious, wary, quiet, firm,
He spent his days in honest toil,
Doing the duty next him found,
Till hour of destiny had come;
And doors were opened, where he walked
To name and place, and heritor
Of brightest crown the century bears.

 From out the soul's mysterious depths,
Whose covered fountains human eye
Hath ne'er explored, springs human thought:
As light doth flow from living flame.
 The soul illumed and filled within,

There breaks upon the waiting ear
A voice, of thought the ripened fruit.
　Thus from the nation's inmost heart,
Torn with her conflicts, pains, and fears,
Beset by fiends who sought her life,
One earnest, solemn word was heard,
Saying to Slavery's maddened hordes:
"Thus far, no farther, shalt thou go."
　And LINCOLN was the nation's voice
Elect unto her highest place.

　The weary months went creeping by,
Until the nation's uttered voice
Could crystallize to legal forms,
And deeds could take the place of words.
　During these months the rebel chiefs,
Unhindered, wrought their treason schemes.
　The arms were stripped from loyal States,
The war ships sent to distant seas,
The nation's treasure-house despoiled,
And every governmental force,
In civil rank, in courts and arms,
Was honey-combed with traitorous men.
　While those who sat in seats of power,
By ones and twos, by tens and scores,
With vapid boast of high intent,
And much pretense of dignity—
But careful still to draw their pay—
They left the nation's capital
Till triumph of their traitor plans
Should give them back their seats again.

　To briefly fill one vacant place,
And hold the keys of treasure vaults,
Whose gold had been by traitors stole
Came one, whose loyal, spotless life
　Was as a glorious shining path,
And from his lips there came a word

Like rifle bullet to its mark,
A bugle blast to loyal men,—
A word which joins the name of DIX
To Freedom's banner evermore:
"If any man attempts to pull down the
American flag, shoot him on the spot."

And while the struggling Ship of State,
Dismantled, scuttled, robbed, and fired,
Abandoned by her traitor crew,
Was tempest-driven o'er the sea,—
The captain daft, by perils crazed,—
Three men clung to her slippery planks,
And held her helm among the rocks,
Until a captain trod her decks
Who dared to face this awful storm;
And 'mong the crowned immortal ones,
The names of STANTON, DIX, and HOLT
Shall shine in glory evermore.

A crowd was gathered in the street;
A citizen who held his home,
And household gods and children's graves,
Within the town, was leaving now.
His neighbors came to say "Good-bye,"
And listen to his farewell words.
He spoke of memories of the past,
And calmly on the future gazed.
"I go," said he, "to meet and share,
Duties and dangers that have come
To none since days of WASHINGTON;
Too weak, these burdens 'lone to bear,
Give me remembrance in your prayers."

Some days had passed. The electric light
Had flamed along his chosen path,
Revealing to the nation's eyes
Triumphant progress day by day,

As crowds had thronged his chariot-wheels,
And waited his inspiring words,
When suddenly the lights were out,
And silence on the heralds fell!
　The league of foul conspirators
Was thwarted in their hellish plans,
While through their thick'ning murd'rous plots,
LINCOLN, unharmed, in safety passed
To portals of the capitol.

　In quiet grandeur sinks the sun,
When regal work each day is done,
And quiet, o'er the eastern hills,
He takes anew the throne he fills.
　No great parade, or vain display,
Enough to be the king of day.
　Thus quiet, on Columbia's shores,
Retiring rulers rest their powers,
And tranquil, noiseless powers arise,
As morning sun illumes the skies.
　No jeweled robes or crowns to wear,
No *vivas* on the perfumed air,
No gilded scepter stained with blood,
No prostrate men in worship bowed;
But simple forms and quiet words,
A sacred oath, a reverent kiss,
A bowéd head, a tear-wet eye,
Thus LINCOLN took his solemn trust,
A nation's welfare to defend,
And execute a nation's laws.

　With solemn oath recorded high,
He stood beneath the open sky.
　Insurgent States around him stood,
Assassins thirsted for his blood,
Dangers were thick on every side,
His instruments as yet untried;
And who was false, or who was true,

Or friend, or foe, he scarcely knew.
Alone! yet not alone was he,
Who rested on Infinity.

No fabled senate of the gods,
Where Jupiter, the first in rank,
Presided at the council board;
No conclave 'mong the spirits lost,
Mourning the splendors from them reft,
And seeking paths by which to rise
To their departed dignities;
No sages found in ancient Greece,
Or senators of conquering Rome,
No patriots of later time,
Who nobly cleft these infant States
From heart of ancient empire—none
Are worthy of a higher rank
Than those who gathered round their chief,
His work and destiny to share,
In this the nation's darkest hour.

First, SEWARD stands; the favorite son
Of Empire State. Twice called to hold
The highest place in her domain,
And thrice sent forth to speak her voice
Within the nation's Senate halls;
Historian, jurist, statesman, sage,
Instructor, leader, neighbor, friend,
A patriot to the inmost core,
To Freedom wedded evermore;
Courteous and quiet, mild, serene,
Amid conflicting passions' flame.

Beneath the tumults of the hour,
Which many used as stepping-stones
To place and gain, he clearly saw
The "Conflict Irrepressible."
And throned above the earthly powers

And principalities, he saw
The "Higher Law," whose restless force
Will break in pieces and destroy
Whate'er withstands its righteous sway.
   He had the art, without offense,
To give a voice to Freedom's hosts;
And while wrong principles were pierced,
No person felt his dagger's point.

   Careful and cool, precise and firm,
No stranger to the schemes of courts,
Well known in lands beyond the seas,
And knowing well their cherished aims;
Selected by the nation's chief,
He spoke her voice to powers afar.
   Far-seeing, he became the eyes
Dangers arising to descry,
And check before they grew to strength.
   Sagacious, strong, he held the helm,
And guided safe the Ship of State
Past all the dangerous foreign reefs.
   And when his noble work was done,
His country saved, his country free,
And seeking respite from his toils,
He journeyed o'er the continents,
The world uncovered as he passed.

   New Hampshire, with her granite hills,
And mountain peaks with snowy crowns,
Gave birth to SALMON PENTLAND CHASE.
   And from her rocky glades and glens,
Her lakes and streams and water-falls,
He caught the air of Freedom's song.
   Trained in her noblest classic halls,
And drinking there the inspiring wine
Which from the ancient fountains flowed,
His soul was fired with Freedom's love,
And courage to maintain her cause.

His opening manhood gave him place
In battle, on the skirmish line,
At *Cincinnati*, city queen.
 Henceforth, where Freedom needed voice,
In courts, to speak for hunted ones,
Who sought escape from Slavery's chain;
In public press, with ringing words,
To strip the glosses from this crime,
And pour a freeman's just rebuke
On its unrighteous, fiendish laws;
In party councils, to prepare
The platform through whose earnest words
Freemen's convictions utterance found;
As ruler of a mighty State,
To build and strengthen Freedom's lines
Against the black, encroaching tide,
Threatening to overwhelm the land;
Or in the Senate halls, to claim
For freedom rightful sovereignty,
The words of CHASE were ever found.

 Upright and strong, his hands unstained,
Girded with righteousness and truth,
With faith in God and faith in right,
He stood, a tower of strength beside
His chief, well chosen for the work.
 And when the storm of war had burst,
Demanding millions day by day,
As ancient Hebrew smote the rock,
And plenteous streams came gushing forth,
So, at his word, the treasure vaults
Poured out exhaustless golden stores.

 Supreme amid the northern seas,
Where slanted sunbeams faintly touch,
When not expelled by Arctic night;
Where rivers turn to frozen plains,
Which fill the valleys with their flow,

And whence are yeaned the iceberg flocks,
On throne of ice, sits giant COLD,
The unconquered king of Arctic climes.
　Whoe'er attempts his realms invade
Are backward turned by crystal bars;
Or, passing through his outward lines,
Are folded in his icy arms,
And sleep the sleep that knows no morn.

　Within his frost-locked fortresses,
And deeply covered magazines,
He stores his arms and drills his troops.
　From thence he sends detachments forth,
Borne forward on the icy blasts;
Sheltered by night they sweep along,
Stripping the earth of all its bloom,
And every glass-blade, every leaf,
Is withered by their chilling touch.
　Where'er is found a water drop,
The liquid diamond turns to stone.
　His legions pierce the solid earth,
And enter rocky crevices,
To rend and lift, to break and crush,
Unchecked by fear, unawed by pain.
　One passion only seems to fill
The soul of this all-conquering king,
Restless, despoiling, crushing force.

　But these invading armies gone,
The earth is softened by their tread;
The rocks are ground for food of herbs,
Budded the bare and lifeless twig,
And harvests new and fresher bloom
Come following in the ice-king's steps.
　And higher wisdom use descries,
And beauty, in these ministries.
　And thus another giant wrought,

Leaving to other servitors
Their healing anodynes to bring.

 EDWIN M'MASTERS STANTON'S name
Was entered on the roll of fame,
Through service in the Union cause.
 His freedom-loving father left
Virginia's Slavery-poisoned soil,
And in *Ohio* found a home.
 From birth, this freedom-scented air,
To STANTON strength and courage gave.
 He walked through academic halls,
And drank from ancient classic lore.
 Girding his loins for earnest work,
He wrestled with the chiefs at law,
And gained in courts an honored name.
 With hardy fiber in his frame,
And firmer fiber in his brain,
In the meridian of his days,
With powers unwasted, eye undimmed,
With heart of oak and will of rock,
He came to do a giant's work
In mastery of giant crime.

 Not first among the chosen few
That waited at the master's side,
But out of time, apostle born;
Yet, coming to the chosen place,
His work was grandest of them all.

 This master passion ruled his life,
To crush the treason-builded State,
And scatter its defiant hosts.
 As ancient prophet broke the calf,
And ground its particles to dust,.
Making its votaries drink the same,
So he, unceasing, sought to break

The gilded idols of their love—
Both Slavery and their ruling power—
And let them drink the bitter cup
Their crimes had mingled for this draught.
. And to this flame-lit passion heat
Was joined a cool, sagacious brain,
Adapting wisely means to ends.

His clarion voice rang far abroad
For men, and men, and still more men;
For arms, and arms, for every arm;
For cartridge, caps, and shells and balls;
For tent and train and boat and bridge ;
For engineers and instruments;
For surgeons, with their medicines;
For food for all the gathering hosts;
For clothing, blankets, knapsacks, shoes;
For pick and shovel, horse and mule,
Saddler and smith and carpenter,
To fashion enginery of war.

And at his call the earth was moved,
The cities poured their treasures forth,
Foundry and loom quick answered back,
Forest and mine sent forth a shout,
The harvest-fields bent low their heads,—
All voices joined, "We come, we come!"
And farm-house, field, and shop and mill,
The lumber camp and darkened mine,
The student's bench, professors' chairs,
Pulpit and press and healing art,
Merchant and clerk and counselor,
Each answered to the patriot call,
And sent their share of living men.
And while these streams were pouring forth,
The cry went echoing through the land,
"Three hundred thousand more we want,"
And soon, "Three hundred thousand more;"

And as these thousands passed along,
Five hundred thousand more may come.
　And STANTON at the gate-way stood,
And day by day he tireless wrought,
Still molding with his iron hands
These men and arms, and stores and trains,
To engines of resistless power,
And millstones of unmeasured weight,
To grind to powder every force
Lifted against his country's flag.
　No taunts, or threats, or smiles, or gibes,
Turned him a moment from his work.
　Where duty placed him, there he stood;
Where duty pointed, he was found.
　An iron pillar, strong was he,
His soul, incarnate energy.

　The shepherd king of Israel
Had next him stand a mighty three,
And after these another class,
Less mighty only than the three,
And WELLS and SMITH and BLAIR and BATES
Beside the burdened Lincoln stood,
Staying his wearied, fainting arms.
　Their work, less shining, quiet wrought,
But needful for the nation still.

XV.

THE EMANCIPATION PROCLAMATION.

THE Hebrews had the Jordan crossed,
The waters fleeing from their feet.
The cloud by day, and fire by night,
Had led them o'er a wondrous path;
Through depth of sea, past Sinai's crests,
The manna for their daily food,
And waters gushing from the rock.
In all their glorious history,
Jehovah had been sword and shield.
With mighty Joshua in the van,
And all their sacred banners lift,
With golden promises aflame,
They started to possess the land.
When lo! their conquering steps were stayed,
And Israel fled before his foes.

The Babylonish garment hid,
With silver shekels, wedge of gold,
Though covered with the soldier's tent,
And further covered in the earth,
Were open to the eyes of God.
And while this crime remained uncleansed,
Unsheltered by Jehovah's power,
They braved the battle strife in vain.

The days were wearing slowly by,
And still the nation's prayers and tears
And sacrifice seemed poured in vain.

The war-clouds still obscured the sky,
Turning the day to midnight gloom,
While toward the nation's capital,
Hosts of defiant rebels pressed.
 And when these foemen crossed their swords,
The Union armies oft were foiled.
 The hope deferred, which maketh sick,
Oft harbinger of early death,
Was pressing hard the nation's heart;
Sick of the dreadful scourge of war,
Filled with its agony and woe,
And sick, to loathing, of the crime,
The poison whence convulsions rose.

 As Atlas bends beneath the world,
Thus burdened is a human soul
Bearing within a mighty thought.
 The painter, in whose soul is hung
A picture, grander, more divine,
Than human fingers yet have traced,
He trembles with the joyful pain.
 The sculptor with his forms unwrought,
The orator with speech unsaid,
The poet with unuttered song,
Which struggles through his meager words
And infelicities to find
Expression worthy of the theme,—
Like loaded wain beneath its sheaves,
Each soul is with its burden pressed.

 And if we may with reverence touch
The tragic scene, and go beside
The sinless One, who walks alone
The dark and sad Gethsemane,—
Whose laboring soul the anguish bears
For all our sinful, sorrowing race,—
And see Him bowed upon the earth,
Moistening its dust with bloody sweat;

We there can learn that inward thought
Both soul and body wrings with pain.

And heavy-burdened is the heart
Which only earthly wisdom knows,
When in its chambers flames a truth
Which, like a sword with double edge,
May thrust our friends, while smiting foes,
When fear and hope, with equal strength,
Menace the unborn mighty word,
Struggling to break its prison walls.

Thus LINCOLN, while the dreadful storm
Of war was raging, fierce and hot,
And burdens crowded all his strength,
Found growing strong within his thoughts
A question, of such vast import,
Reaching so far, so deep, so high,
Touching so many interests
Of peace and war and government,
Of time and life and destiny,
Of untold millions yet unborn,—
Question whose umpirage depends
On powers and possibilities
Of moral and material force,
Which human wisdom may not gauge,
Or sound their vast, unfathomed depths.

The hot breath from the cannons' lips
Had shriveled all the legal forms
Oppression had so deftly wrought.
Writs and attachments lose their force
Where laws are framed by bayonets;
Superior force, or Power divine,
Must stay his hands whose will directs
The marshaled armies in their might.

And thus, our LINCOLN held the key

Which now could open prison doors.
   Should he, or should he not? The key
Was in his hand; the door was near;
Should he throw back those massive bolts,
And widely swing those iron doors,
And to the millions there enchained
Pronounce the God-like words, "Be free?"

   The inward battles of the soul
Are only by experience known;
And only LINCOLN knew the heat
And fierceness of the fire he passed.
   Not strange, he trembled with the weight
That day and night upon him pressed.
   Not strange, there gathered all the powers
Of earth, each clamoring for his ear,
That some should crowd him toward the brink,
While others held him back in fear.
   Not strange, that heaven and hell should strive,
Where such momentous issues joined.
   Not strange, he sometimes felt the need,
In droll, grotesque, and strange conceits,
To change the currents of his thoughts,
As birth-pangs leave some moments' ease.

   When woodman's ax, with blow on blow,
Has laid the forest monarch low,
With wedge and maul he rives apart
The gnarled and twisted fibrous heart.
   The sharpened wedge at first is set,
Then lightly tapped with beetle weight,
Till firmly in its place 'tis fixed,
When heavy blows descending swift,
The thick'ning wedge is homeward sent,
And long compacted grain is rent.
   And LINCOLN, in his early days,

"Rail splitter" called, had learned the ways
Of woodcraft. Never butt of wedge,
But always use the sharpened edge.

At first proposals, quiet made,
To grant assistance to such State
As would emancipate its slaves.
The words seemed of but little worth,
And most but small attention gave.
But those who watched, with eyes alert,
For signs, observed the sharpened edge,
And saw the flashing of the steel.
From time to time, repeated strokes
Fastened secure the tapering wedge,
Whose entrance, forced by mighty blows,
Should rive, from out the nation's heart,
The black and poisonous Slavery growth.

Appointed chiefs had often led
Their armies 'gainst the rebel lines,
And met repulse. Then broken ranks
Were closed and filled, and struck again,
And backward still again were rolled.
Anon the line of battle changed,
Rebellion, proud, defiant, bold,
Its cohorts fiercely northward rolled,
Potomac crossed, and *Antietam*
Had turned their banners south again.
While armies thus in bloody strife
Contended for the nation's life,
The conflict raging in the breast
Of LINCOLN came to final rest.
On bended knees, this solemn word
Had record there before the Lord:
When rebels southward should be driven,
The mighty word, as voiced from heaven,
Should echo forth from sea to sea,
"The chains are broken, men are free!"

The President his council called;
Grave questions oft before them came,
Testing their wisdom. Oft perplexed,
They careful studied every point,
The threat'ning dangers to avert.
And oft each gazed in other's eyes,
To read the fears they never spoke.
While gathered thus, the President
A scroll unrolled and quiet read.
Not filled, as roll the prophet saw,
With lamentation, mourning, woe,
But in those technic, measured words,
And through those harsh and jagged lines,
Was shining forth a glorious light,
Which seemed like rising of the sun
That ushers in millennial morn.
Their purpose plain, direct, and strong,
And rising to the lofty heights
Of manhood, freedom, conscience, right,
They thrilled these sages as a peal
From resurrection angel's trump,
Commanding dead men, "Rise, and live!"
Unconscious rising from their seats,
Their flashing eyes and close-pressed lips
Revealed emotions seldom stirred.
Suggestion as to form and word
And time were sought, and closely scanned;
But none had a dissenting voice
Against the purpose written there.

When delegates from nascent States
Sought liberty from foreign rule,
They chose their foremost man to draft
The declaration of their wrongs.
With careful phrase and studied art,
Embellishment and ornament,
He wrought the story of their woes;
Declaring truths but dimly seen,

In words so luminous and bright,
That burdened nations sang for joy
This new evangel of their rights.
   And while the ages pass along,
The facile pen and glowing tongue
Shall o'er and o'er repeat again
These burning words to listening men.

   But LINCOLN's word of liberty
Was dry and hard. It had a sound
Like cannon drawn o'er rocky road ;
A clang of rifles, cartridge box,
Or click of bayonet set in place ;
Like military order drawn
To build a fort or bridge a stream.
   But reading through the dreary lines,
Explaining purpose, setting forth
The ends for which the war was waged,
Defining limits, marking bounds,
Reciting statutes Congress passed,
We meet these soul-inspiring words:
"ON NEW YEAR'S DAY, OF SIXTY-THREE,
ALL PERSONS HELD AS SLAVES SHALL BE
THEN AND THENCEFORTH FOREVER FREE."

   The word went forth. The lightnings flashed
The blazing symbols o'er the earth.
   The winds and waves took up the sound,
While Freedom's trumpets shouted forth,
"The year of jubilee has come !"
   Like burst of sunshine in the storm,
To freedom-loving hearts it came,
Making their love of liberty
And patriot love a single flame ;
The electric spark which forces joined
Inseparable evermore.
   And through the hoary prison walls
It pierced the dungeon vaults, illumed

The eyes so long in darkness kept,
Showing its freedom-kindled fire,
As spectroscopic lines declare
The metals burning in the sun.
    One chance remained for rebel States
To save their treason-breeding crime.
    But still the adage kept its truth,
" Whom gods destroy they first make mad."
    Yet vain and proud and arrogant,
Withstanding still the nation's arms,
They scoffed a proffer which proposed
Submission to the Union laws.

    The brave, intrepid Corsican,
Who dashed through thrones and dynasties
Like blazing comet through the skies,
In atheistic blindness said,
"The side of Providence is where
The heaviest cannon sweeps the field."
    But morning sun of Waterloo
Was hidden by the falling showers,
And o'er the soft and slippery plains
The heaviest cannon could not move,
While Blucher's troops came marching on,
To thwart his hoped-for victory.

    And States and people, who had crushed
The men in God's own image made,
Were blinded by their dreadful crime,
And only saw their human foe.
    Anointed eyes alone could see
Chariot and horse of flaming fire,
And Union forces joining rank
With longer lines of heavenly powers,
Whose armies fill the earth and skies.
    No need henceforth to blindly ask
Where God is found amid the strife.
    The Union arms, to Freedom joined,

Alliance made with Him who came
The bruised to heal, th' enslaved to free.

A hundred days were quickly passed,
And day of destiny drew nigh.
Day of delight to those in chains,
Who waited for the final blow
To burst the fetters from their limbs.
A dawn whose breaking light dispelled
Two hundred years of darkest night
For Afric's bleeding exile sons.
But day of darkness, day of doom,
To builders of the Babel schemes,
Who sought to rise above the heavens,
And overmatch Jehovah's power.

The morning came. The word renewed
Cut the last cord of Federal law
That bound the nation to this curse;
Took the last sheathing from the sword,
Which henceforth, double-edged, should strike
Both Slav'ry and secession 'like.

The word went forth, not borne alone
By human lips and human hands,
But angel voices sang again,
In richer chorus, Bethlehem's strain,
"Glory to God, good-will to men."
And He who walked amid the storm,
On raging waves of Galilee,
Again repeated, "I am here,
Mighty to save; be not afraid!
I now make bare th' Almighty arm,
I come to whet my glittering sword,
And answer now the long-groaned prayer
Of the oppressed for liberty."
And in the cabins of the poor

There shone a brightness as the sun,
And voices shouted, " Freedom's come."

    Ten thousand households bowed in prayer,
Returning thanks to see the day
For which so long they hoped and prayed.
    And dying saint, with blood-washed robes,
Passing a conqueror through the floods,
Victor o'er sin and death; her soul
Had caught the airs of Paradise,
And saw by faith the heavenly ones,
Yet waited still to hear below
The word which set the captives free.
    Unto her dying bed was brought
The sacred words. She heard them read,
Her soul took in the mighty truth,
And, using failing voice, she cried,
" Glory to God! Amen!" and died.

XVI.

THE BATTLE STRIFE CONTINUED.

WHEN, molded in th' Almighty hand,
The earth was formed, of sea and land,
And continents and oceans shone,
Each belted with its varied zone,
And mountain ranges reared their crowns,
While valleys sloped in beauty down,
And o'er the vast capacious plains
Ran rivers filled with falling rains;
No spot or place, o'er all the earth,
From east to west, from south to north,
Showed more of beauty, grandeur, power,
Creation's bright consummate flower,
Than gathers in the wondrous tale
Of mighty Mississippi vale.
   For ages Adam's wandering sons
With restless foot have walked the earth,
Seeking the long-lost Paradise
Of which the soul has memories.
   But thorn and thistle, rock and sand,
Still bruised their feet and pierced their hand;
Bowed down by labor's heavy load,
While earth, reluctant, gave them food,
They sought through Asia's vast retreats,
From arctic snows to torrid heats,
And over Europe's mountains high,
And Afric's deserts bare and dry,
To find the vale, in vision blest,
Where burdened, wandering man might rest.

And through the weary centuries
This vale in virgin beauty lay;
From ancient lust of empire kept
By distance and the ocean deeps,
And by its coastwise mountains hid
From ravishment by brigand States,
When first the Atlantic waves were crossed.
  A vale of beauty, stretching far,
From northern table lakes and lands
To tropic air, and spreading forth
From east to west an emerald sea,
The glory of the continent.

  From mountain torrents, dashing down
Through labyrinths of glens and vales
On western Alleghany slopes,
The waters swift to rivers grow;
Where trade and travel, hand in hand,
Through mountain passes find their way,
Till, joining in their onward flow,
La belle rivière! the beautiful
And broad Ohio sweeps along.
  Thence onward for a thousand miles
The silver ribbon westward runs;
While southward from alluvial plains,
Where rising empires gird their loins,
And northward from the mountain heights
Great rivers joyous greetings bring,
Giving their floating palaces
To join the enchanted moving throngs
Which dance in triumph o'er its waves.

  And when these thousand miles are passed,
Father of Waters meets our gaze,
Thence northward for two thousand miles,
Where rising States and rolling streams
O'erwhelm our fainting, burdened thought;
Or westward for three thousand miles,

Along Missouri's turbid flow,
Where empires slumber yet unborn,
And mountain streams, now dancing free,
Shall sing with hum of rolling wheels,
And earth that waits the tiller's toil
Shall groan with burdening grains and fruit.

O, matchless vale! a restless world
Is pressing toward thy fond embrace;
Thy vast, capacious plains and heights
Two hundred million souls doth wait;
Thy soil, with generous fullness blest,
Hath food for nations, far and nigh;
Thy mountains fringed with oak and pine,
Thy valleys blushing with the vine,
Thy seas of coal and streams of oil,
Copper and lead and iron ores,
Silver and gold in bounteous stores,
Are waiting labor's magic touch,
Which shall transform thy ancient night
To paradise of morning light.

And when the gauge of battle, thrown,
Proposed to place in foreign rule
This river in its southward flow,
The dwellers in this wondrous vale,
O'er all their hills and harvest plains,
And cities growing by their streams,
Gave forth this changeless, stern decree:
"While waters fill our flowing streams,
And seek an ocean outlet free,
As long as cities dot our plains,
Or commerce rides on ocean wave,
So long shall those who till our fields,
And yearly sing our harvest songs,
Have open pathway to the sea."

And when upon the river's bank

Were cannon mounted to dispute
Their passage o'er these waters free,
Each mountain stream and rivulet
Sent with its waters living men,
Still singing, in their onward flow,
"As mountain springs our streams renew,
So youthful hearts, as strong and true
As those who now are pouring forth,
Shall rise afresh from virgin earth,
And onward roll both night and day
Till every barrier shall give way,
And from its sources to the sea
The Mississippi shall be free."

These flowing streams of living men
First struck Confederate walls in gray
In *West Virginia*. Pouring on,
Led by M'CLELLAN and ROSECRANS,
They swept *Rich Mountain, Carrick's Ford*,
And from rebellion cleansed these lands.
Another stream, whose banners bore
Symbolic name for Freedom's hosts,
FREMONT, the leader of free men,
O'erflowed *Missouri's* troubled fields,
And LYON, SIGEL, CURTISS, BLAIR,
At *Jackson, Carthage, Wilson's Creek*,
At *Sugar Creek* and at *Pea Ridge*,
Led the advance of Freedom's lines,
And crowding back the lines of gray,
The State was left in Union hands.

And still the rising stream rolled on,
Turning its central 'whelming tides
Toward fortresses on river banks.
Fort Henry and *Fort Donaldson*,
Shiloh and *Corinth*, in their turn,
Were each o'erwhelmed and overborne.
Belmont, New Madrid, Number Ten,

And *Memphis* next were grandly won;
When, looming up, defiant, bold,
Vicksburg was found across their path.

While these events were passing by,
Each step contested to the death,
Another living stream had found
Its way unto the river's mouth.
    Led by the gallant FARRAGUT,
Son both of Neptune and of Mars,
His squadron swept away its foes,
Forced the surrender of the forts,
And anchored at the city's side.
    And BUTLER, never knowing fear,
Took up the reins of guiding power,
And order reigned in *New Orleans*,
Chief city of the rebel States.
    The fiery dragons swept away
All batteries from the river banks,
Save *Vicksburg* and *Port Hudson's* guns.

While we for re-enforcements wait,
Let us one actor briefly sketch.
    ULYSSES SIMPSON GRANT was born
In *Clermont* County, *Ohio*,
In eighteen hundred twenty-two.
    The subtle forces of the soul
Sometimes reveal themselves in tests
More delicate than chemists' use.
    The story of the Trojan war
The winter evenings occupied
Of pioneer in western wilds.
    Among the heroes of that strife
One chief his admiration gained.
    His words well fitted to their place,
Sagacious as to means employed,
Fearless as death and brave as right,
Rising in resource and in power

As difficulties barred his way,
Cool both in vict'ry and defeat,
And silent when he should not speak.

 And when an infant son appeared,
Not strange ULYSSES was his name,
Nor strange the hidden stream of life
The forces bore from sire to son,
Which swam in his admiring thought.
 The impulse, from which sprang the name,
Inspired the father to secure
His son's adoption by the State,
And as the nation's foster child
His hands were trained to smite her foes.
 The soldier's formal drill complete,
In Mexico 'twas put in use;
And following there the stripes and stars
O'er battle-crimsoned, conquering fields,
He won promotion in the strife.
 Some years in camp in times of peace
The unused sword was placed in sheath;
Surrendered were his martial trusts,
With men he took a toiler's place.
 But booming guns at *Sumter's* side,
Trained on the banner of his love,
Aroused him from his peaceful dreams,
And with the gathering hosts he came
Responsive to his country's call.

 The florist in the early spring,
Conning his stock of seeds and bulbs,
Knows not from which shall spring the flower
Whose radiant charms shall crown the field.
 So in the gathering hosts of men
No human eye could there discern
The coming leader of the host.
 The sunlight, air, and rain from heaven
Were given free alike to all.

But some grew quick in length of stalk,
And gave large promise in their leaf;
They budded fair, but slowly flowered,
And faded soon. But men for crowns
Need more than promise of the leaf,
Or half-formed buds upon the stalk.
   They need the fragrance of their deeds
To crown the glory of the flower.
   And our ULYSSES, while unknown,
Put on the glory of his deeds;
And when his name was wafted far
It gave a fragrance to the air,
And freshness of the early bloom
Through summer's burning sun increased,
And sweeter fragrance still arose
Through autumn's storms and winter's snows.

   And earnest work had won the name
Of UNCONDITIONAL SURRENDER GRANT,
Before he led his soldiers forth
To wrestle with the wide-spread floods,
The wilderness of slough and swamp,
Malaria, fever, chills, and death,
Earth-works and mines, abatis, pits,
Mortar and Parrott, rifled guns,
Bayonet and bomb, and singing ball,
And battering-rams, and ships of fire;
These joined with ranks of iron men
Contending, as they long were taught,
Against the spoiler of their homes.

   With these our hero problems found,
And tests for courage, patience, faith.
   From side to side he vainly sought
To break an entrance through these walls.
   Approaching armies for relief
Were overmarched and overmatched,
And fought, and scattered to the winds.

And when the storming column failed,
Beat back by walls of rock and fire,
Then earth was made to challenge earth,
And rifle-pit watched rifle-pit,
While mine was countervailed by mine,
And with the modern arts of war,
Like maddened mastiff, in his rage,
He closed his jaws on neck of foe,
Nor blows, nor blindness, pain nor death,
Could break his ever-tight'ning hold.

While holding thus his struggling foe,
The copperheads, from out their holes,
Lifted their heads and fiercely hissed,
And shot their slimy poison forth;
But yet from loyal footsteps shrank,
And dodged into their holes again.
Prophets of ruin trumpets blew,
And tried to set anarchic fires,
To call the soldiers from their work.

But still this earnest, silent man
Wrapped arms of iron round his foe,
Nor loosed one fiber of his grasp,
Until the fainting form gave way.
And on the nation's natal day
The starry flag was lifted o'er
The mighty fortress, and the streams
Of flowing waters, flowing men,
Unvexed, rolled onward to the sea.

For three successive years the strife
Along the broad Atlantic slope
In fierceness raged. Rebellion, proud,
Had brought her governmental forms,
And reared aloft her serpent crest
Near to the nation's capital;
And *Richmond* challenged *Washington*.

And from these hostile fountains flowed
The forces, which, in battle joined,
Crimsoned the silvery waters' flow,
Through broad and beauteous *Chesapeake*,
The central gate-way of the land.

At *Baltimore* fresh loyal blood,
From *Massachusetts* soldiers drawn,
Was spattered on the stony streets,
And, washed by falling rains, it stained
The flowing *Susquehanna's* tide.
This blood, so rich in loyal strain,
That each infinitesimal drop,
Not only stained the waters' flow,
But sprinkled many million hearts,
Anointing them for holy work.
Potomac had her bloody chrism
Repeated oft. *Bull Run*, *Ball's Bluff*,
And *Antietam*, with *Gettysburg*,
Each gave its field a crimson blush,
To moisten dusty track of death.
And *Shenandoah*, mountain stream,
From *Harper's Ferry* to its source,
Was often stained with crimson hues,
While storms of iron rain and fire
Rolled back and forth. At *Winchester*,
Front Royal, *Cross Keys*, *Shepherdstown*,
From time to time the storm-cloud burst.
And *Rappahannock*, *Rapidan*,
Pamunkey, *Chickahominy*,
And *York*, and *James*, each in their turn,
Were witnesses of battle-shock,
Where tens of thousands gave their lives.

And when these bloody years were past,
Each hostile power defiant stood,
And seeking still its early goal.
Rebellion sought for *Washington*,

To crowd its treason-founded State
Within the nation's capital,
And thus to show a waiting world
Attempted revolution gained,
And crime and violence enthroned,
With Slavery as a corner-stone.

And *Washington* still *Richmond* sought,
Sending her loyal legions forth
To spoil the nest where Slavery hatched
Her viperous brood, and crush the powers
That warmed the serpents into life;
And bury in a common grave
Both Slavery and his treason-child.
Freedom and Slavery, ancient foes,
Incarnate now in governments,
In marshaled armies, ships, and forts,
Powder and ball, and glittering steel,
Are face to face in battle joined,
And each intent to kill his foe.
Freedom, in robes of righteousness,
With eyes of light, with hands unstained
By wrong; with sympathy for man
In every clime; unprejudiced
By accident of race, or name,
Or birth, or color of the skin,
But standing on the word divine,
With clarion voice aloud repeats,
" God of one blood hath made all men,"
And all alike his laws embrace.
Yet now her robes are powder-stained,
The blood is dripping from her hands,
Her eyes are flashing battle-fires,
And every muscle tense to pain.

While Slavery, with his bloody fangs,
And hoarse with shouting his commands,
By Freedom's sword is brought to bay.

Surprised, enraged, his tiger-threats
Gleam fiercely in his savage eyes;
His blackened robes in tatters torn,
And through his gaping wounds the life,
In crimson floods, is pouring forth;
Yet, blinded by his rage and crime,
He presses still the awful strife.
And o'er the mountains, rivers, plains,
Through fields and forests, cities fair,
By road and bridge, and wall and wood,
Trampling with feet of blood and fire,
These giants wrestled each for life;
Not yet decided who shall die.

Again the winter solstice past,
The sun creeps up the southern sky.
Again the nation girds her loins
To prosecute long-baffled work.
A captain to the front has come,
With "swing of conquest" in his tread.
With powers enlarged, and force increased,
Lieutenants chosen at his will,
Modest and brave in like degree,
Union and law his guiding stars,
Content to do a soldier's work,
He quietly assumes command;
And at his word the legions move,
Seven hundred thousand men in arms.

The opening spring of sixty-four
Revealed this battle line: the left
Resting upon the Atlantic shore;
Thence westward to the mountain heights,
South-westward o'er their rocky crests,
To *Chattanooga, Tennessee;*
Thence west to Mississippi's floods,
And down the same unto the gulf.
The plan was made to pierce this line

Upon its center; thence to swing
The Union column to the coast;
Thence turning north along the shore,
To flank the rebels from their holds,
And meeting then the advancing left,
To crush rebellion in its folds.
   The work alone the plan revealed.
   To lead this column to success
The fitting man was quickly found.

   Tecumseh! Indian warrior, chief,
Statesman and brave, of Shawnee tribe,
Ohio born, when manhood came,
Was leader in the chronic wars,
By which the Indian sought to stay
Encroachments on his forest home.
   The scattered tribes by him were joined,
And with his flaming passions fired.
   Tippecanoe their power broke,
But failed to crush Tecumseh's will.
   A new alliance 'gainst his foes
Brought to his aid the English arms,
And many years his name and fame
Was ringing through the western wilds.

   Ohio judge of early time,
Who bore an honored brightening name,
Admiring saw the brighter traits
Which graced and crowned the Indian chief,
Beneath his rough and rugged life:
His love of country, love of race,
His broad and comprehensive plans,
Persistence, courage, bravery, faith,
Which under Homer's glowing song
Had robed him with immortal fame.

   And when another human flower
Bloomed on the flowing stream of life,
Shaded and colored by the soils

O'er which the fecund waters flowed,
The father, wisely, gladly wrote
WILLIAM TECUMSEH SHERMAN'S name.

With one of nature's noblemen
His early orphaned years were spent.
Beneath that kindly guiding hand
Life's subtle forces were inspired,
And later youthful ardor sought
A training in the art of arms.
A time he bore the nation's sword,
Then turned aside to civic arts,
Till Slavery into treason riped,
At the meridian of his days.
The call for Union volunteers
Found SHERMAN promptly in the field;
And early in the bloody strife,
His clearer vision plainly saw
The mighty struggle which had dawned.
Some blinded ones thought him insane,
But later learned his head was cool,
And judgment less than need required.
The conflicts of the passing years
Had proved the temper of his steel,
And garnished his unsullied sword
With shining wreaths of victory.

With preparation duly made,
His columns were in motion set.
One hundred miles of mountain paths,
Through forests, ravines, rocks, and swamps,
With armies holding every pass,
The bridges from the rivers torn,
Was first installment of their work.
But feeling at the guiding rein
The pressure of a steady hand,
Voiding obstructions of the way,
They moved with confidence and power.

On right and left, by front and flank,
The armies couching in their path,
From time to time were backward turned;
Till SHERMAN, with exultant host,
Had swept the mountains of his foes,
And held *Atlanta* as his prize.
The central city of the South,
The heart from which the blood went forth,
Where treason forged the shot and shell
Which turned their southern lands to hell,
This city of the mountain lands
Was clasped in loyal Union hands.

A brief respite from soldier toils,
As eagle folds his bloody wings,
Returning from the wild foray
To shelter 'mid the mountain crags.
With ruffled plumage quickly cleansed,
And beak and talons burnished new,
The daring eye peers through the haze,
The soul is thrilled with sense of wings,
And stretching forth his royal neck,
He rises toward the stormy sky,
Away, away from human sight.
Thus with the soldier of our song:
He drew his columns to his side,
Folded apace his weary wings,
And washed the powder stains away.
Then, loosened from his mountain perch,
He soon was lost to anxious sight.

The boatman at the river's side,
When called to cross the swollen tide,
'Mid floating spars and sunken rocks,
Where treacherous currents sweep and swirl,
While storms and darkness, dangers hide
Is followed by our anxious fears.

And as we stand, with straining eyes,
Trying to pierce the darkened veil,
And only see the foaming wave,
And hear the waters' sullen roar,
Fearing the boatman's sinking cry;
Then, as the welcome signal-light
Flashes its rays from farther shore,
A weight is lifted from the soul.
  Or when the dying saint has passed
Beyond the sights and sounds of earth,
While laboring through the mortal strife,
He sends the pressure of the hand,
Or joyous flash of dying eye,
To signal to these mortal shores
The visions of eternal life,
Our sorrows are illumed with joy.

  And thus the loyal millions wait,
While SHERMAN and the Union host
Pass through the long and darkened night;
Pass through the heart of rebel lands,
Surrounded by their maddened hordes,
Until the thunder of their guns
We hear along the Atlantic shore;
Until the gleaming of their swords
Has flashed dismay in rebel forts;
And soon, before their conquering tread,
The rebel flag has bowed in shame,
And o'er M'ALLISTER's walls and guns
Was lifted to the morning light
The glorious ensign of the free,
And SHERMAN's march has reached the sea.
  As divers seek for hidden gems
To grace and crown a beauty's charms,
Savannah was a Christmas gift,
A pearl, brought from the ocean drift,
Once torn from Union diadem,
By SHERMAN set in place again.

While this eventful march progressed,
A rebel captain led his arms
Northward, to lure the conqueror back,
But failed his 'tent. And *Nashville* saw
His columns shattered at her gates,
By Thomas made a broken wreck.

But time and language fail to tell
Of camp and march and battle storm,
Where skirmishes Marengoes were,
And minor battles Waterloos,
Where, by arbitrament of war,
And judgments written down in blood,
Questions of empire, rule, and race,
For continents, and destinies,
For centuries were weighed and fixed.
Only the headlands of the shore,
Or mountain peaks of wide-spread lands,
Are seen at once by human eyes.
The closer view but segments take
Of circles reaching far from sight.
A few of these attention claim.

XVII.
RETRIBUTIVE JUSTICE ON CITIES AND LANDS.

WHEN Israel stood with trembling awe
    Before the mountain swathed in fire,
    Whose crown was dark with blinding light,
When herald thunders ceased their roar,
There came to shuddering ears of men,
In awful voice, the law divine;
Jehovah's changeless words of truth:
"For I, Jehovah, God most high,
Am jealous for my holy name,
And all iniquity I mark,
And judgment give in sure return;
As fathers sow their sons shall reap,
In generations yet unborn,
Of those who spurn my righteous laws."

    And earth, through all her weary years,
Bears witness to the avenging rod;
Since first she felt the primal curse,
The woes that come of human sin.
    Swept by the all-engulfing flood,
Salted with Sodom's rain of fire,
And sunken underneath the sea;
By earthquakes rent, volcanic storms
Pouring their floods of molten fire,
And burying cities at their feet.

And barren rock and burning sand,
Where verdure once the landscape crowned,
All mark God's overflowing wrath
Toward those whose sins defy his power.
 Though scoffers in their venom rage,
Their unbelief shall never make
The word of God of none effect.

 Cities are centers, whither flow
People and wealth of border realms.
 Cities are eyes; adjoining lands
Through these behold the outer world,
Shaded and colored by their hue.
 Cities are fountains, sending forth
The streams which bear their full-brimmed life
To fertilize surrounding fields.
 Cities are indices of powers,
And Paris is France in many lands.

 And *Charleston* was the focal orb,
The index city of the South.
 Her merchants, envious, madly sought
Commercial empire; vainly talked
Of grass-grown streets, deserted wharves,
When fullness of commercial life
Should crowd her harbors and her marts
With trade her rivals once controlled.
 Her dwellers swung their beavers high
When LINCOLN was the people's choice,
A pretext given now to rend
The Union bonds. For decades gone
Treason here bubbled hot and fierce,
And ever threatening overflow;
Secession's fountain, here unsealed,
Flowed onward like an earthquake wave;
And here the maddened, murderous wrath
Broke forth against the nation's life
In torrents of consuming fire.

And when the day of judgment came,
And wrathful angels, gathering nigh,
Their vials poured on earth and air,
Then earth belched forth avenging flame
Which *Charleston* drank in iron rain;
Then air put on her wings of fire,
Sweeping o'er palace, mart, and spire,
And when from fiery kiss released,
Charleston was found a blackened corse.

Columbia also, capital,
Was joined with *Charleston* in her crimes;
Within her legislative halls
The treason factions had been nursed.
And here convention first had met
And passed resolve to break the bonds
That bound her to her sister States,
And then to *Charleston* had adjourned
To consummate their chosen work.

When SHERMAN's soldiers, tramping on,
Set rebel armies all in flight,
As rabbits fly the hunter's steps,
Leaving *Columbia* crazed with fear,
They threw some brands on cotton bales
To save their idols from their foes.
The angels of the air arose
And blew these sparks to quenchless flames,
And cotton, long their pride and boast,
Became to them a Nemesis robe,
Woven a fiery winding-sheet.

A bright and sunny autumn day
Within the Shenandoah vale,
Beneath the peaceful open sky,
Surrounded by the stubble fields,
Where bounteous harvests had been reaped,
An aged man was brought to die.
Long lines of soldiers filled the plain,

With shotted guns and bayonet set,
While trembled with a nameless fear
All actors in that tragic scene,
Save him who come to taste of death.
 His step was like a conqueror's tread;
His brow was radiant as a crown;
His work, thus far, he thought well done.
 Pinioned and blinded; cart and rope,
And accidents of time and place,
Were only palings by the way
Through which he passed to angel powers.
 Henceforth, released from earthly clod,
He freedom gained of earth and heaven.
 But where he stood, and how he fell,
Pursued to death by hounds of hell,
Was written in the books of God,
Recording angels witnesses.

 The earth twice passed her yearly round
When spores of blood that filled the ground
A harvest brought. And through that vale,
And up its mountain sides and glens,
The fields were filled with arméd men.
 And as these armies trampled forth,
From North to South, from South to North,
The song was floating on the air,
Mingled with drum and trumpet blare,
With smoke of burning towns and mills,
With cannon boom and bursting shells,
With bullets falling like the rain
On harvest field and grassy plain,
With corpses o'er the hill-side strewn;
The song still rose of "Old JOHN BROWN,
Whose body moldering in the grave,
His spirit still kept marching on."

 One further instance we recite,
Where judgment angels walked the earth.

The poison-plant on Freedom's soil
Was planted first beside the James.
From thence the deadly fungus spread,
Clothing a continent in shame;
And threatening speedy overthrow
Of struggling Freedom's final hope.
And when the land refused increase,
Blasted with barrenness and death,
God's image then was there debased
And bred like brutes for public sale.

But when the Sodom grapes were ripe,
And reapers, with their sickles sharp,
Gathered the clusters swift and clean
For wine-press of Jehovah's wrath,
Whence blood to horses' bridles came;
Not strange, where first the poison grew
The judgment angels should be sent,
And that *Virginia's* towns and plains
Were swept by God's avenging fires.

Thus do the unseen Powers regard
Those who contemn their righteous laws,
And unseen forces sleepless wait
These holy laws to vindicate.

XVIII.

NEGRO SOLDIERS: PRISONERS OF WAR.

WITH all the savagery of war,
  Among the nations Christian termed,
  Some points of honor are maintained.
In fiercest conflicts, flag of white,
Or banners furled, or arms reversed,
Demands surcease of deathly blows,
And foes surrendered kinsmen are.
  The savage only tortures those
Whom war delivers to his hand.
  But in this struggle, which comprised
Revolt from the advancing light,
Lifting the earth to higher plane,
These codes were often set aside.
  Rebellion meant perpetual crime
And slavery till the end of time;
And as the conflict waxed more fierce,
And need had come for every arm,
Or white or black, to help to save
The Union ark, which jewel held
Of freedom for both black and white,
And colored men, with flashing eyes,
Were gladly rushing to the front
This precious jewel to preserve,
Rebellion's highest counsels said,
"Hang every man that leads the blacks,"
And whispers went through all the land,
To blacks no quarter should be given.
  These counsels had but small avail,

For those who led and those who fought
Had watch-word, " Victory or death,"
And first or last they seldom failed.

Fort Pillow stains historic page,
And stained the spirit of the age,
Where soldiers, laying down their arms,
Were met with savage massacre.
 The wondrous mechanism of life
In some was velvet-robed, in some
Their vesture was of parchment made;
But each was met with murderous hate:
The first, because they dared to fight,
Their right as freemen to maintain;
The latter, though their color white,
They dared to own their brothers men.

Beneath the open wintry sky,
Within inclosure, roughly formed
By palisade and open ditch,
A bound within as dead-line known,
With gate-ways barred and rifle guards,
And canister to sweep the field;
Within these lines of bristling steel
Were held ten thousand Union men.
 Their shelter was but ragged tent,
Or earth-bank raised to shield from wind,
Or excavation in the ground,
Where men, like beasts, gregarious slept.
 Of clothing robbed, and in its stead
The shreds of what were garments once,
Or cast-off rags of enemies.
 Their food unwholesome, coarse, unclean,
From which decaying odors rose;
Too meager to sustain their life,
Had it been suited to their needs.

The men who passed these horrid scenes

Had come from cheerful, pleasant homes,
And wealth and station some had known,—
From village beauty, farm-house filled
With plenty, loving hearts, more dear
Than all the world beside; from homes
Where prayer was offered, praise arose,
Where art and taste and culture reigned;
The Christian church and school, and all
The sweet amenities of life.

And these now walked the prison pens,
By malice made starvation dens;
There, ragged, freezing, starving, passed
The weary wintry days and nights;
There fought the demons till their hair
Was bleached to whiteness in their prime,
Till maniac drivel, idiot's stare
Looked forth where once was reason's throne;
Till hunger, gnawing through the frame,
Had eat the muscles from the bones;
Till staring eyeballs, scarcely held
In sunken sockets, ghastly shone;
And skin, from former measure shrank,
The hunger-sharpened jaws revealed.

These famine-stricken skeletons,
Like specters, walked among the graves,
And dreamily as dazed, they talked
About "God's country" whence they came,
Contrasting in their wearied minds
The visions of the shining past
With earthly hell which round them closed,
And mingling hopes of heavenly bliss
With memories of earthly homes.
And specter angels with them walked,
Servants of death, of many names,
Consumptions, fevers, flux, and chills,

Whose slightest touch would rend apart
The fretted cordage, which had held
Body and soul in living bonds.
 Thus Union men, as prisoners held,
Were starved and froze, inviting Death
To sign their papers of discharge,
Or else return them to their ranks,
Unfit for soldier-service more.
 Not one alone, Golgotha thus,
But every southern prison place
Of these sad horrors had its fill.

 Among the mountain slopes of land,
Jagged and broken, which divide
The waters reaching Delaware
From those to Susquehanna turned,
In central part of Empire State,
Two boys had passed their mortal birth,
The entrance gate-way to the earth.
 Their parents were by blood allied,
And lived contiguous each to each,
And boys, so near of equal age,
Were playmates from their infant years.
 The passing seasons changes brought,
The lads were growing tall and fair,
And summer toil on rugged farms
Was alternate with winter school,
With moon-lit sleigh rides, paring-bees,
Which youths and maidens ever please,
While mingled with the mirth and noise,
These brown-haired, blue-eyed, restless boys,
The crowning joys of homes they blest,
With filial and fraternal grace.
 And when our father ABRAHAM, pressed
With care to fill his wasting ranks,
Sent far abroad the clarion cry,
"Five hundred thousand more we need,"
The boys gave heed; then counsel took,

And then resolved to bear a part
To keep their priceless heritage,
And Country, Union, Freedom save.

 They started forth. Their fathers' prayers
And mothers' tears, the benison
They bore, to cheer them in their work.
 With velvet softness on their cheeks,
And ruby their unrazored lips,
The types of purity and truth,
And faithfulness, they bore within.
 As man is lost without a name,
We publish, free from stain or shame,
KIRBY DEVOL, the first in years,
And THEODORE CAMPBELL, worthy peers;
Then side by side in rank they stood,
With lifted hands they firmly swore
Faithful to serve their country's flag;
Then where it led they followed on,
Through weary march and battle-storm.

 A rebel swirl at *Cedar Creek!*
Surprised! surrounded! ranks unformed,
With empty hands, no chance to flee,
And they were prisoners to their foes.
 The days of weary march had end
At *Saulsbury's* deathly prison pen.

 These boys, by tender mothers kept,
Sheltered and clothed in pleasant homes,
From bounteous tables daily fed,
And warmed by cheerful blazing fires,
Had changed from all these sweet delights
To horrors 'mid tormenting fiends.
 But courage, lads; all is not lost;
Exchange may come; the war will end;
" God's country " you may see again.

The soul of man by guilt unstained,
By black despair is never chained,
And from the lowest depths arise
Some rays of hope which reach the skies,
Lifting the soul from earthly clod
To praise and fellowship with God.
  And gleams of light the darkness veined,
The soul uplift by inward strength,
With courage faced opposing foes.

But hunger, loneliness, and cold
Were constant factors of their state,
Which they could ne'er eliminate
From the dark problem of their lives.
  And courage, bravery, hope, and faith
Were yielding to their crushing power;
As elemental wars corrode,
And gravitating force beats down
The proudest monuments of men.
  Diseased, despairing, homesick, starved,
With death in all its protean forms
Gnawing asunder cords of life,
A way to escape the fangs of death
Was opened to these suffering ones.

The strains of martial music caught
And captive held their listening ears,
Recruiting sergeant in the camp,
The rebel banner o'er him borne.
  To starving ones he promised bread,
And clothing for their naked limbs,
Largess of money, for the needs
Of all who joined their conquering arms.
  And some in weakness took the bribe,
And moved by fear they purchased life.
  But Satan's lie proved false again,
And many came from humble homes
Who never give their all for life.

"We talked it over." Council of war
In desp'rate straits. "And we resolved
Rather to die than break our oath."

And one came back, pallid and waste,
With ruined health, to tell the tale;
And one—his starved and wasted form
Sleeps with the thousands who have gone
To nameless graves, their land to save.
But yielding thus his mortal life,
Keeping unstained the priceless pearl
Of truth,—swearing and changing not,
Death's portals passed; a radiant crown
Adorns his brow, and Holy Hill
Welcomes another conqueror home.

Beside these shining ones we place
The civil leader of the South,
And captain of their martial hosts,
Who, raised to name and place and fame,
Through freedom favoring Union laws,
Lifted their parricidal hands
Against the land that gave them life;
With broken oaths upon their lips,
And Slavery's poison at their hearts,
Went forth to fill the land with slain;
To kindle blazing, bloody flames,
The Union temple to consume;
And in its place to build a tomb
To bury Freedom's only hope.
When judgment scales are even set,
"Tekel" shall brand these falling stars,
Though weighted but by beardless boys.

XIX

CONTINUED STRIFE.

THE rolling, restless wheels of time
　Their steady motion forward keep,
Bearing along the untraveled track
Earth's dwellers, to their final home;
Nor aught of human joy or pain
Check them a moment in their course.
　The storms may sweep o'er land and sea,
Volcanoes belch their floods of flame,
And earthquakes rend the continents;
Famine and pestilence devour,
And war with breath of fire consume;
Empires and dynasties dissolve;
But 'mid confusion, change, and death,
The wheels of time serenely roll.
　The great sun swings, still back and forth,
From north to south, from south to north,
While index finger slowly points
The cycles of the universe.

　Returning spring of sixty-four,
Found armies of the East once more
With faces toward *Richmond* turned.
　Three years had passed, and frequent change
Of leaders to these arms had come,
And each assayed to pierce the walls
Of living men that blocked the paths
Which reach the rebel capital;
And shattered, broken, each had failed.

Through *North Virginia's* tangled fields,
By *Rappahannock, Rapidan*,
Through *Fredericksburg* and *Chancellorsville*,
Culpepper, Spottsylvania,
The legions trampled back and forth,
Obscured by clouds of dust and smoke,
To music of the screaming shells,
And singing Minies' warning note,
Commingled with the cannon crash;
Till roads and runs and glens and crests,
With fen and forest, field and farm,
Were crimsoned each with flowing blood,
And yielded harvests of the dead.

Another captain, leader now,
Laureled and crowned from conflicts fierce,
Who oft forced victory from defeat.
The bitter strife again renewed,
GRANT pushed across the *Rapidan*,
And in the tangled wilderness,
Grappled anew with ancient foe.
Six days and nights the conflict raged,
Shaking the earth and darkening heaven.
Like mammoth serpents stretched afar,
Whose every part was poisonous fang,
And forkéd tongue and barbéd sting
Were darting forth on every side,
While fold on fold of scaly mail
Had covered every vital part
Which each in vain assayed to find.
Or, like unyielding living walls,
Which were by mighty powers uplift,
And dashed together, face to face,
Till crimson torrents swiftly poured,
While northward flowed a stream of blue,
And southward ran a line of gray,
The refuse from the wine-press crush.
But still these armies kept their place,

The lines of gray unbroken stood;
And ranks of blue had southward turned,
No more their footsteps to retrace.

The word went forth, "By left flank, march!"
And from the tangled wilderness
The living wall was forward moved,
To meet on *Spottsylvania* heights
The extended line they long had fought.
Another dash of wall on wall;
Severe the shock; but neither fall.
Again the word, "By left flank, march!"
And next *North Anna's* bloody fields,
Where neither to the other yields.
And still the word, "By left flank, march!"
And then *Cold Harbor's* fiery rain,
Where *Gaines' Mill* was fought again,
And soil, once wet with loyal blood,
Again was crimsoned by its flood,
While mighty blows of Union hands
Still failed to break the rebel bands.
Once more the word, "By left flank, march!"
And when the river James was crossed,
And northward turned the Union host,
The iron men, whose battle brunt
They oft had met, were still in front.

And still these walls in fury dashed,
Like ocean waves by tempests lashed,
And cannon crash and scream of shell,
Of harvest fields made earthly hell.
Yet each position still maintained,
While summer into autumn waned,
And autumn changed to winter sere,
Companion of the dying year.

Contemporary with these scenes,
The skirts of these contending foes

Were oft in fiercest conflict joined;
At *Wytheville, Lynchburg, Frederick,*
And rebels threatening Washington,
Then forced again to southern fields,
And *Martinsburg* and *Chambersburg*
Had each their chrism of blood and fire.

   And then was found the long-sought man,
In person of PHIL. SHERIDAN,
A compound formed of brains and fire,
With bone and muscle made of wire,
Whose royal presence brought relief,
Like bugle-blast of Scottish chief,
And sword-gleam flashing swift and free,
Was as a shout of victory!
While clangor of his horse's feet,
Changed mad advance to swift retreat.
   Then quickly followed *Opequan,*
Which told the temper of the man,
And rebel prowess, strength, and skill
Was overmatched at *Fisher's Hill;*
Then *Cedar Creek,* with Union rout,
Was quickly, grandly, turned about,
And evening saw victorious feet,
Where morning met so sore defeat;
And rebel banner nevermore
Was lifted on the *Shenandoah.*

   Another wing swept down the coast,
And TERRY led the Union host
Through surf and sand, o'er bog and mire,
Through storm of enfilading fire,
And over *Fisher's* crest of flame
They onward swept like falling rain,
And halted not their conquering bands
Till foes were prisoners in their hands.
   Then through this newly opened road
SCHOFIELD's victorious legions trod,

And captured *Wilmington* once more
The loyal Union banner bore.

Another corps, with webbéd feet,
Led by the gallant FARRAGUT,
Had walked the waters of the gulf,
And entrance sought to *Mobile Bay*.
  The pass was overhung with forts,
Which stood like lions by the way,
With lips drawn back from iron teeth,
While monsters mailed, and steel-clad rams,
With mortars spouting liquid fire,
Joined with torpedoes 'neath the wave,
Combined to stay their onward course.
  But heeding naught they onward pressed,
Commander in the fore-top lashed.
  They grappled with their numerous foes,
And worsted each on sea and land,
Till over *Mobile's* towers and forts
The starry banner proudly floats.

And WILSON, with his thundering tread,
Through northern *Alabama* swept;
Selma was won; *Columbia* next;
Then *Chattahoochee; Macon* came;
And arsenals and armaments,
And magazines of shot and shell,
And factories, where these tools were wrought,
Were taken from the rebel hands,
Crushed and despoiled for future use;
While cotton, by the thousand bales,
Was food for the devouring flames.

The end is nigh! it hasteth on!
The starry banner, trailed in shame,
Is lifted to its place again,
And in its beauty proudly floats
O'er all the sea-coast towns and forts.

The bugle blasts of Freedom's hosts
Have echoed through the southern land.
  Their towns have seen the boys in blue
Victorious marching through their streets;
And muskets borne by swarthy hands,
With steady feet and flashing eyes,
Have opened to the dullest sense,
That old foundations are destroyed.

  While thus the Nation struggling held
The precious jewels of her love:
Union and Freedom, Law and Right;
With every muscle tensely strung,
And all her soul with anguish wrung,
Bathing her brow with bloody sweat,
The time returned, when ruling powers
Must render back their sacred trusts,
And struggling, bleeding, suffering men
Must sit in judgment on their acts.

  Then from their hiding places came
Prophets of foul and hateful mien,
Blazing their treason burdens forth.
  Some worshiped still their party gods,
And sought to reinstate in power
The party chiefs, whose sympathies
Were with rebellious States in arms.
  And some were filled with such contempt,
Such maddened scorn of colored men,—
To wrest from these their new-born hopes,
And weld their half-dissevered chains,—
These joined their efforts to defeat
Those who had promised Freedom's dower;
Choosing to sink the ship of State,
With priceless treasures all on board,
Lest black men share these precious gifts.
  And some had wearied of the strife.

And some, despairing, only saw
A rebel triumph in the end.
And debt was piling mountains high,
And gaping wounds were bleeding fresh,
While wailing woe was bursting forth,
Like that which ancient Egypt heard,
When every house contained its dead.

But through this mazy, tangled web,
Woven of passions, fears, and pain,
There ran broad bands of shining gold.
Heroic purpose; firm resolve;
Unswerving fealty to the right.
With single eye and steady aim,
Their bodies thus illumed with light,
Came Freedom's millions to the fray.

From stormy, rock-bound coast of *Maine*,
To *California's* golden shore,
From silver lakes, from central plains,
From mountain height and vale and town,
The bugles brought them to their camps,
With Freedom's trustiest weapon armed.
And through the day their mighty blows
Were falling like the drifting snows;
And when the day of strife was done,
And Freedom's battle grandly won,
The wondering nations saw the choice,
And heard the echo of that voice,
Which, louder than the thunder's roar,
Proclaimed afar from shore to shore:
"If all our treasure be the price,
And streams of blood the sacrifice,
From northern frost-bound inland seas,
To bloom and fruit of orange-trees,
From morning light to set of sun,
The land we love shall still be one."

The rebels saw these drifting snows,
Hiding from sight the Union foes,
Crushing, beyond all power to help,
The left wing of their allied hosts,
And saw therein their hastening doom.
   The judgment record of this court
Declared to those in power: "Well done,
Proceed and close thy appointed work."

XX.
THE FINAL VICTORY—THE REJOICING.

THE April ides again approached.
    Four years had passed, historic years,
    Since bloody sword was first unsheathed,
Which drenched the lands in crimson floods.
    Wisdom of ancient time hath said:
"Let him who girds his armor on,
Boast not as if the strife were won."
    In opening chapters of this strife
Treason was proud, defiant, bold,
While those who met this fierce array,
Came slow and trembling to the work.
    The blood of Teuton tribes is cool,
But warmed in war's hot crucible,
It holds its heat like molten rock.
    Through slowly passing wintry months,
The Union captain pressed his lines
Against the lengthy, living walls
That girt the rebel capital;
Holding these soldiers in their place,
Till SHERMAN's hosts had clove in twain
The remnant of the treason band.
    And through the wide Confederate States,
Tornado like, the Union arms
Resistless swept away their foes.

    The time had come. Again the word,
"By left-flank, march!" and living wall
Stretched onward 'round the rebel right,

Doubling it back upon itself;
While on the long-extended line,
Which the beleaguered cities joined, .
The Union thunders burst in storm.

A Sabbath morning dawned on earth,
And brazen-throated, clanging bells
Had summoned earthly worshipers
Once more to meet in house of prayer.
 Within palatial *Richmond* church
The rebel chief in quiet sat.
 Unheralded, a messenger
Came tramping through the lengthened aisle,
And halting at his crimson seat,
Delivered message to his hands.
 The words were few, but big with fate;
His captain said: " My lines are broke,
And *Richmond* must be left to-night."
 The assembly felt an awful hush!
While every eye was turned on him
Who rose and left the house. Fit act
To close the drama of his power.
 A dream of empire, which began
By crushing out the rights of man,
And trampling on the higher laws,
Which flow from the Eternal Cause;
The path Apollyon early trod,
Symboled by leaving house of God.

Thy dream is past, the play is done,
And daylight pales thy tinsel crown.
 No more shall nations trembling stand
Appalled by thy audacious hand.
 No more shall cringing courtiers fear,
Nor flattering *vivas* reach thine ear;
But worlds beneath thy coming wait
With taunt and jeer to curse thy fate;

A morning star, once robed in light,
Now fallen to perpetual night.

Last struggle now!—a race for life,
Leaving the lines so firmly held,
The rebel arms assembled swift
And started on their western way.
With broken lines came broken hopes,
Ill-armed, ill-clad, and starving now,
Hoping alone to find some path
T' escape the conquering victors' tread.
While GRANT, who watched with eagle-eye,
Descried his now-uncovered prey,
And swooped his legions on his foes.
Upon the left, to lead the van,
The bold and fearless SHERIDAN,
Whose troopers cut their fleeing lines,
And bayonet points their columns turned;
Wasting their thin and shattered ranks,
While captive thousands were his prize.
And on their rear the gallant MEADE,
Who won his crown at *Gettysburg*,
Pressed and retarded them in flight.

Another Sabbath morning dawned,
Their fleeing columns, struggling on,
Had *Appomattox Court-house* gained.
And here, deployed across their path,
A line of cavalry was found,
Who firmly held their chosen ground.
And when they swung to right and left,
And formed to dash on rebel flanks,
The gleam of countless bayonets met
The vision of the weary host,
From which, despairing, they recoiled.

And ere the Sabbath sun had set,
The army, which so long had stood

Rebellion's last and greatest hope,
Whose blood had wet so many fields,
Who bravely suffered, bravely fought,
With courage nobler than their cause,
Bearing their proud untarnished name,
"*Northern Virginia,*" ceased to be.
  Their captains and their broken hosts
Were prisoners, held by Union hands.

  Flash! lightnings, flash! with speed o'ermatch,
The rays of morning as they flash;
Haste! haste! along thy iron way,
Nor let thy burning coursers stay,
But drop from off thy flaming pen,
On mountain, plain, and vale and glen,
In teeming cities by the sea,
And forest homes of industry,
The words for which men watch and pray,
And hungry wait from day to day,
And spread afar o'er land and sea
The news of Union victory.

  Ring! joy bells, ring! and as ye swing
The victory tell with louder ring;
Let steeple voices laugh and shout,
Tossing their wild huzzas about;
Let court-house, school, and hall and tower,
Swing hallelujahs hour by hour;
Let every brazen tongue rejoice,
And tell its joys with loudest voice.
  Ring! joy bells, ring! and chiming sing
The airs of freedom while ye ring.

  Scream! engines, scream! for once let steam
Burst forth, and fill the land with scream;
Let shop and mill, from vale and hill,
Scream out their joy with glad good-will;
Let every prow that plows the sea

Scream out its joyous ecstasy;
Let iron horses in their might
Go screaming forth their wild delight;
From city, village, hamlet, town,
From mines and mountains, up and down,
Wherever iron muscles move,
Responsive to the breath they love,
On land or sea, by shore or stream,
Let engines scream, and scream, and scream.

Boom! cannons, boom! for once there's room
To thunder forth thy notes of doom.
Rebellion's dead, of Slavery born,
For them no resurrection morn;
Let iron lips their gladness pour,
And speak their joys with endless roar.

Wave! banners, wave! no more shall slave
E'er groan beneath thy banners' wave;
Lift up thy shining folds on high,
And rapturous kiss the morning sky;
Let every flag-staff in the land,
With glory crowned, triumphant stand;
No rival flag disputes thy claim,
Or dims the brilliance of thy fame.
Thy union blue and shining stars
Remain unmarred by wounds or scars;
Thy battle-stripes of flaming red
Have holy memories of the dead;
While Peace and Freedom, Truth and Right,
Are mirrored by thy snowy white.
Then upward climb to loftiest height,
And freely float in wild delight;
With all thy glorious blended hues,
Proclaim afar the joyful news:
The battle strife at last is done,
And final victory is won.

Shout! freemen, shout! ring bravely out
Such tones as only freemen shout;
The finger silent on the mouth,
No more shall symbol North or South,
Nor men need speak with bated breath,
Lest utterance seal their lips in death.
But pen and press, through all the land,
With speaking voice and artist's hand,
Through chiseled marble, picture rare,
And song and story, bright and fair,
May lift the burning truth on high,
And write it broadcast o'er the sky,
The devils dumb are now cast out,
And children healed may freely shout.

Sing! minstrels, sing! loud praises ring,
And songs and anthems joyous sing.
Let earthly hallelujahs rise,
And meet the chorus of the skies;
Timbrel and harp take up the strain,
All voices join in rich refrain,
To tell the triumphs of the Lord,
His glorious victories record;
Rider and horse are in the sea,
The Lord hath triumphed gloriously;
While on the shore his chosen stand,
Saved by his own Almighty hand,
With loud acclaim repeat the song,
While heaven and earth his praise prolong.

Weep! maiden, weep! for joy so deep,
Thy brimming eyes can never keep;
Thy heart was with the weary march,
And sentry's lonely midnight watch;
'Twas caught within the fearful crash
Of charging columns' wildest dash;
'Twas often pierced and wrung with pain
By whistling Minies' leaden rain;

It courage gave when soldier pressed
O'er fiery rampart's bloody crest;
In love and honor sacred borne,
With joy its bearer shall return;
And, freed henceforth from war's alarms,
Shall gladly clasp thee in his arms.
 Then, maiden, weep! thy joy so deep,
Thy brimming eyes no more can keep.

 Blaze! beacons, blaze! rejoicing raise
From height to height continuous blaze,
Till every mountain-top shall stand
A flaming signal to the land,
That Treason, from her guilty throne,
By righteous judgment is cast down;
War's bloody tramp o'er earth shall cease,
And in her place walk white-robed Peace.

Shine! cities, shine! for miles in line,
Let all thy lights in splendor shine;
While mounting high from base to dome,
Thy storied windows burst in bloom;
And every casement, every tower,
Pour floods of joy on midnight hour,
And symbol forth the Nation's night,
Now changed to glorious shining light.

 Speak! patriot, speak! or strong or weak,
The joy that thrills thy being speak;
Let statesmen, from the Senate halls,
Responsive meet the Nation's calls;
Let orator, with silver tongue,
And poesy, with glowing song;
Let ermined jurist, from his seat,
And learners, waiting at his feet;
Let those who truths divine declare,
And sacred robes devoutly wear;
Let yeoman, tiller of the lands,

And artisan, with horny hands;
Let trembling age, with palsied tongue,
And youth, with passion flaming strong;
Let each speak forth with soulful voice,
And all harmonious loud rejoice.
  The mighty from their seats are hurled
To realms of darkness under-world;
The babel tower, on which they wrought,
And building high, they vainly sought
To stay the rising floods of light,
And empire keep of ancient night,
By Power divine is overthrown,
And sinks beneath the depths as stone.
  Thus driven from the face of day,
Workers and work all swept away,
Lines of confusion strew the ground,
And stones of emptiness are found.

  Rest! soldier, rest! the crucial test
Now passed, assures a soldier's rest;
For years but little respite came
From labor to thy burdened frame.
  How oft the weary march was thine,
Holding thy place in wasting line!
  How oft on midnight watch alone,
Hiding behind a tree or stone,
Or lying on the open plain,
Exposed to frost or falling rain,
When burdened, weary, hungry, weak,
Then rushed along at double quick;
Scorched by the sun's devouring rays,
Pressed to the front in battle blaze;
By wounds and sickness sorely tried,
Thy comrades falling at thy side;
These weary years all now are passed,
And rest has come to thee at last.
  Thy bronzed and battered features bear
The impress of terrific war.

Enduring purpose, firm-set will,
Through all defeats unconquered still;
Till now thy work is nobly done,
For thee now waits thy early home,
Thy friends and loved ones there to meet,
And quiet rest thy aching feet.

Thy fallen comrades rest have found
On fame's eternal camping ground,
While waits for thee in coming days,
Thy country's grateful meed of praise.

And when the battle-field of strife
Is closed, which ends with mortal life,
May morning roll-call, prompt and clear,
Have victor brother's answer, "Here."

Rest! soldier, rest! with victory blest—
Enjoy henceforth an honored rest.

And broken, bleeding, hapless ones,
Unknown, except as Afric's sons,
Though western born, denied a place
Among the proud Caucasian race;
For centuries scourged and peeled and trod,
By tyrants deemed accursed of God.

Thine hour has come! The morning light
Has dawned on thy perpetual night;
Thy LINCOLN's words of freedom feel,
The Union victory's crowning seal;
And soon these shining words shall trace
The nation's Charter's honored place,
And stand, unchallenged, till the day
When heaven and earth shall pass away.

Thine hour has come! Thy voices raise,
And strike the highest chords of praise.

With songs and shouts and flowing tears,
And hopes triumphant o'er thy fears,
Lift thy unshackled hands on high,
And joyous clasp the azure sky.

Embrace the earth, the light, the air,

And all their new-born glories share;
Reach upward, where the burning sun
Resplendent sits his flaming throne,
And feel thou art a brother born
To stars, who sang Creation's morn.
  Before thy now unpinioned feet
The highways rise, serene and sweet,
And leading from thy lowly lot,
Through every path of human thought,
Till mountains scaled and oceans crossed—
By storm and tempest fiercely tossed—
Thy soul, redeemed from earthly curse,
Finds freedom of the universe;
No more a thrall, but hence a man,
A part of God's eternal plan.

  Thine hour has come! to lead the song,
And fill thy shouts with passion strong.
  While others sing exultant strains,
Thy voice has tones of breaking chains;
While others sing of victories won,
Thy songs proclaim oppression gone;
While others sing of country great,
Of peace and union in the State,
Thy higher note is, MEN are FREE,
And blood hath purchased LIBERTY.

XXI.

DEATH OF LINCOLN.

HUSH! joy bells, hush! Let silence fall
Like funeral pall o'er stricken land.
   A mortal paleness overspreads
Each cheek and brow late flushed with joy.
   Let breaking hearts pour out their sighs,
And songs give place to anguished groans,
While sorrow's tears, like falling rain,
Are shed o'er Israel's beauty slain.

   LINCOLN has fallen! victory crowned,
And robed in Freedom's spotless white,
Jeweled with justice, truth, and love.
   Fallen, while wearied heart and brain
Was planning mercy for his foes.
   Not fallen from his high estate
Of matchless purity and truth.
   No stain hath touched his toiling hands,
No darkness veiled his moral sense,
No shadows dimmed his vision clear
Of human right. The bitter strife
Hath ne'er his spirit's sweetness marred.
   His soul hath never felt the touch
Of vanity, or pride of place,
Or mad ambition's baleful fires,
Which patriots oft to Cæsars change.
   But in the zenith of his fame,
In fullness of his rounded powers,

Rebellion's dying struggles struck
A blow which reached his mortal life.

And through the Nation's jubilant song
A tone of quivering anguish ran,
And joy was turned to dark despair.
And skies were draped in funeral gloom,
The noon-day sun was black and cold,
The air was thick with deathly fume,
The wind went murmuring through the pines,
So sad and dreary, lone and chill,
It froze the currents of the soul.
And men, like specters, slowly moved
With muffled drums and sorrowing dirge,
And banners overlaid with crape,
To listen to the soulless words
Which heavy dropped from chalky lips.
LINCOLN was dead! and other souls,
Benumbed with fear, dead also seemed.
Dead! by the mad assassin's hand,
Who, trained and taught in Slavery's school,
Saw swift dissolving all their power,
As Slavery's empire crumbled down
Before the tread of Freedom's hosts.

As when the storm had overpast,
And forest trees and harvest fields
Were prostrate in its angry wrath;
When storm-cloud slow retired from view,
And muttering thunders died away,
While sunlight on the landscape fell;
From depth of dark sulphureous cloud,
Into the sunshine sweet and still,
There leaped a wrathful flaming shaft,
Which sought and quenched a precious life.
And in that house which held its dead
The sweetened air and sunlight clean
Was naught in presence of their pain.

And when our noble LINCOLN fell,
Slain by Rebellion's dying throes,
In presence of the mighty dead
The land burst forth in wails of woe.

And of the willing instrument,
Who sought immortal infamy
By blackest crime the century knows,—
Like rabid dog pursued to death,
Let name and memory rot unknown.
As worlds in endless circles run,
Bringing the seasons in their course,
By the Eternal order held;
So worlds of human passion find
The curb and reign of righteous law,
Repeating ancient days once more;
And ere the oppressed find liberty
The dead are found in every house,
From dunghill peasant to the throne.

And LINCOLN! prophet, statesman, sage,
Leader and captain of the host,
Bearing with patience, strifes, and fears,
From barren lands producing bread,
And water from the rocky wastes;
From victory's mountain heights he saw,
But never trod, the promised land.
As prophet, from his lips had come:
"Jehovah's righteous laws may claim,
For every drop of precious blood
Wrung by the lash from Afric's sons,
An even drop, drawn by the sword,
Shall flow from the oppressor's veins,
For just and true are all His ways."

And when the cup was even set,
And brimming full of precious blood,
It needed still another drop

To balance all the overflow
Two hundred years of crime had wrought.
   And to the saddening dirge, which rose
O'er fathers, husbands, brothers, sons,
From North and South, in stricken land,
As the death-angel reaped his sheaves
From many bloody harvest fields,
Was given added notes of pain
When LINCOLN fell among the slain;
Who, at the closing of the strife,
To crown his labor gave his life,
Our times' great name, by wide consent,
Our Freedom martyr President.

XXII.

PUNISHMENT OF REBELLION.

TWO brigand chiefs in days gone by,
Who found a home in Italy,
Behind her northern mountain bars,
And hidden by her crags and spars,
Despotic ruled the murderous clans
Which gathered in their secret dens.
  One was soft-spoken, pleasant, fair,
And polish had of modern air;
He knew the ways of easy speech,
And oft of right did loudly preach;
On those he met he blandly smiled,
And thus with courteous art beguiled.

  The other was of coarser mold,
And added to his love for gold
Was written on his hardened face
The brutal passions of our race,
While crime and lust and every vice
Seemed lurking in his demon eyes.
  These captains kept their clans apart,
Though they were closely joined in heart.
  The one still talked of human right,
As noble, godlike, in his sight;
While other ever argued still
For full dominion of the will.
  But when the hour of pillage came
Their modes of action were the same;

With fire and sword they battled still,
The one for right, the one for will.

Upon Italia's sunny plain,
Surrounded by the golden grain,
And softly fanned by summer breeze,
Which whispers through the orchard trees,
A villa stands. Its rural homes,
Its shops and towers and spreading domes,
Its flowing stream and rumbling mill,
With ancient castle on the hill,
When gleaming in the morning light,
Made picture pleasant to the sight;
And brigand chiefs, with longing eyes,
Were gazing on this golden prize.

From mountain fastnesses then came
These hordes, devouring like a flame;
With sword and ax and battle brand
They spread dismay throughout the land.
But yeomen from the harvest lands,
And laborers with calloused hands,
With villagers from shop and mill,
And armed retainers from the hill,
All bared their arms in battle strife,
For friends and homes laid down their life.

The conflict ends. The hordes are foiled
By men who fought for home despoiled;
Their blows which fell like falling rain,
With dead and wounded strewed the plain,
And chiefs, who led these murderous bands,
Had justice met by vengeful hands.

How sad the story of our race
Since conflicts of the earliest born
Gave promise of a world of strife.
Man seeks companionship in man,

Then struggles for the ruling place,
And earth is deluged with the blood
Shed to obtain or retain power.

And through the vengeful ages past,
Revolt against established rule,
Failing intent, was met by death.

Rulers have claimed that public health
And private welfare were secured
By quenching treason fires in blood,
Before the conflagration spread;
And thus were others timely warned
Before they had the death-line crossed.

But battle-fields are sometimes filled
With warring forces, which, unseen,
Have yet a more persistent life
Than mailed and harnessed living men.

Men are the bubbles of an hour,
Ideas retain controlling power;
They lead as captains in the strife,
Which would destroy a nation's life.

Ideas are brave, and full of hope
They seldom count opposing foes.

But bravest captains sometimes find
Their Waterloo; and glowing hope
Is gloomed with clouds of black despair.

The winds stay not incoming tides,
And stars their endless courses keep,
Though hidden for an hour from sight
By angry storm-cloud in the sky.

Through bloody strife so fiercely fought,
Two captains led the rebel hosts.

The one was proudly State-Rights named,
For him supreme command was claimed.

He bold affirmed each separate State
Retained the power to break at will
The Union bond, and thus destroy
What all had wrought for good of all.

With air of innocence he stood,
Contending that his schemes were good,
And Nation ne'er could use its might
To thwart his theories of right.

The other, Slavery, led the van
In crushing out the rights of man.
Though second named, the real head,
He bold, relentless, brutal, led;
While to his proud imperious sway
All other forces soon gave way.
These captains led the hosts. All else
Subalterns were, and only served
Like hands on dial, turning round
And pointing where the maker willed.
The army heroes, civic stars,
Were only blazonry of rank;
Ribbons and spangles which adorned
Those who these captains humblest served.

When battle strife at last was done,
And Union victory was won;
When white-robed Justice came to call
Transgressors to her judgment hall,
And find the authors of the guilt,
For seas of blood so vainly spilt,
The guilty captains that we name
Were found among the heaps of slain,
Dead! and forever dead they lay,
For them no resurrection day.

The festering corpse of Slavery shed
A stench so foul that those he led,
Now from his baleful power set free,
Turned from the sickening sight away.
And State-Rights, fallen on the field,
No longer now his aim concealed;
But, through his cloak and visor rent,

The nations saw his true intent,
To found an empire, mold a crown,
And Slavery seat upon the throne.
   And Justice, noting where they lay,
She turned her sharpened sword away;
Subalterns share the victor's grace,
When leaders have been shot to death.

   These captains dead, the way is clear
For better leaders in the land.
   A true "State-Rights" shall recognize
Relations to the Union bonds,
Where every State a jewel shines
In circlets of a common crown.
   And guarding every local right,
With sister States a phalanx forms,
Giving the strength of all to each;
Securing thus a sure defense
From foes without, and foes within.

   And Slavery, buried from our sight,
Freedom henceforth shall lead the hosts.
   With port erect and brow serene,
With loving eye and helping hand,
For men of every race and hue,
His sword now resting in its sheath,
And powder stains all washed away,
He walks o'er all Columbia's shores,
And greeting friends, or recent foes,
Is welcomed by them all with joy.

www.ingramcontent.com/pod-product-compliance
Lightning Source LLC
Chambersburg PA
CBHW031946230426
43672CB00010B/2070